UPGRADED

HOW THE INTERNET HAS
MODERNISED THE HUMAN RACE

Published by
LID Publishing Ltd.
One Adam Street, London. WC2N 6LE

31 West 34th Street, 8th Floor, Suite 8004
New York, NY 10001, US

info@lidpublishing.com
www.lidpublishing.com

A member of:

BPR
Business Publishers Roundtable

www.businesspublishersroundtable.com

© Andy Law 2016
© LID Publishing Ltd. 2016

Printed in Great Britain by TJ International
ISBN: 978-1-907794-61-2

Cover and page design: Caroline Li

ANDY LAW

UPGRADED

HOW THE INTERNET HAS
MODERNISED THE HUMAN RACE

LONDON   MONTERREY
MADRID   SHANGHAI
MEXICO CITY   BOGOTA
NEW YORK   BUENOS AIRES
BARCELONA   SAN FRANCISCO

For Alessandra, Tom, Livy,
Venetia, and Matteo

ACKNOWLEDGEMENTS

Thank you.

Thank you to the many people I have met, listened to, and talked with.

This book is an accumulation of contributions from so many people, it is almost impossible to credit everyone.

But I can name a few. Thank you to my wife, Alessandra, for opening my mind to the infinite possibilities of the internet and gathering front-line evidence showing how people are both challenged and changed by it. Thank you also for shining a light on how the internet allows unique and special disciplines to learn from one other, grow, and eventually create new and exciting areas of discovery – ones not previously foreseen. And thank you for reading early drafts of this book, turning them upside down and inside out, and putting them back together almost without my noticing it. The improvements you made are invaluable.

Our children added so much and surprised me too often.

Thank you to my son Tom, who was four years old when the internet arrived and has grown naturally with it since, profiting from all the wonderful changes it brought. You showed me how to forge (and fake) identities and how to marshal the web into an opportunity for work. And you demonstrated that creativity is still a fine art, although technology can upgrade skill sets and shortcut many (previously) professional products and services.

Thank you to my daughter Livy, who will always be the same age as the internet. Where it goes, you will go. How it changes, you will change. Livy demonstrates effortlessly how digital aptitude extends and expands all the accidental opportunities that others might not see.

And thank you, Venetia – you arrived five years after the internet arrived. By the time you turned ten, social networking was commonplace. You do it all now: blog, surf, seek, chat. In fact, you totally exist on the net. It has become an innate part of you – as it is, in different ways, a part of all of us.

It is a cliché now to say, "To understand modern technology you have to ask a ten-year-old." But I did. Thank you, Matteo, for educating me about the deeper mysteries of Minecraft, PewDiePie, and Syndicate, and for living the life of a unique individual with a private, rude, dangerous, and oftentimes totally impenetrable virtual world of your own. You have shown me that youth is reborn through the internet and is no longer an unfavourable clash of middle age past experience and youthful recent discovery.

Thank you Vint Cerf, truly "one of the fathers of the internet." Hearing Vint talk about the interplanetary internet was the slap in the face that reminded me we are at the dawn of all things net-based.

Many colleagues and friends helped focus my thinking. Without them, I would not have understood the unbelievably important and valuable legacy of the pre-internet software industry[1]; or the dramatic implications of "Block-chain", which is writing the fourth chapter of the internet even as I write the first section of this book[2]; or the new models of transactions occurring in public and private networks; or, indeed, the compelling rise, after so many years and many false starts, of augmented, virtual and mixed reality technology, robotics, and artificial intelligence, which are now intersecting with the internet and producing breathtaking results.

Thanks particularly to Adrian Leu, who added important perspectives on some of the critical developments I mention. And to Michael Bayler, who first spoke to me about "reverse networks" and opened many windows into many aspects of "life under the net".

Many thanks, as ever, to Martin Liu, my agent and editor who – five books later – keeps telling me I can write!

And enormous gratitude to the hundreds of people whose materials I have read over the past two years – you have informed this book and filled in valuable gaps.

You know who you are.

CONTENTS

YOU CANNOT WRITE ABOUT THE INTERNET

You cannot write about the internet. It is the internet that now writes about us. It creates the leitmotif for all our lives. It has become our memory, our communication, and our social and commercial behaviour.

This book has never caught up with the changes the internet has brought. The day after it went to print, *something else significant happened in cyberspace.*

This book sits between two others: *Implosion* a review of the impact of the first twenty years of the internet, and *the third book in the trilogy*, which looks at the changing social, physical, and cultural landscape that the internet will engender over the next twenty years. Am I crystal-ball gazing? Well, surprisingly, you can predict fairly accurately what's coming next. It is one of the crazier aspects of the internet. You can predict it because so much of what the internet confers is simple facilitation. If we can think of what we could enable, then the internet, more or less, can facilitate it. We'll see that HG Wells, Marshall McLuhan, and Alvin Toffler got it very right – a very long time ago. Their predictions were spookily uncanny. In 1938, HG Wells predicted that one day everybody in the world would own a radio. These billions of radios would receive and *broadcast* transmissions. All the received and sent transmissions would crisscross over each other like a net, forming a "World Brain" that holds all knowledge and alerts everyone to important news.

In 1966, Marshall McLuhan accurately predicted on-line commerce. He saw the obvious possibility of people transacting with stores electronically and ordering goods and services directly, using the telephone and Xerox, without leaving home.

Alvin Toffler foresaw the world of an internet-enabled life in his startlingly prescient book, *Future Shock*, which was published in 1970. Toffler argued that society was undergoing an enormous

The internet was predicted almost 90 years ago.

structural change, a revolution from an industrial society to a "super-industrial society." Ten years later, in *The Third Wave*, Toffler coined the word "prosumer". He predicted a world in which the personalization of products, in a new contract between consumer and producer, would become possible.

Our human response to the helter-skelter, crazy, wild, phenomenal change that we have brought upon ourselves is one of love, hate, enjoyment, frustration, fear, experience, communication and betterment.

So this book has to be a measured observation. Just as the internet writes our lives, so it also writes itself – every nanosecond of the day.

Undeniably, the internet raises a growing number of questions.

What is it like having an elder of our human tribe (i.e., Google) who is invisible, not human, and not at all a god?

This elder answers all the questions we might want to ask about the lives we lead.

We have elevated knowledge to a higher, grander level. We rarely question the answers we find online. And unlike the Delphic or Sibylline oracles of the Greeks and Romans, we are not in awe of the immense power that comes, ultimately, at our fingertips.

Have we formed an emotional connection to this elder such that the attachment is strong enough for us to mourn its loss? Or do we not see the power Google offers? Instead we experience the power it facilitates and it is we who feel empowered. We have the power. We have enhanced ability.

Do we like this power?

> The internet is moving faster than anything else we have created.

Do we understand how the speed of response and transactions effect us?

The internet is moving faster than anything else we have created. Are we developing fast enough to keep up with the new abilities we have been given?

The changes that have happened in the months since I started this book are breathtaking in the speed, surprise, and distinction of their arrival.

The data and examples I use evidence my remarks, but can never tell the whole story. If you like, this book is a snapshot of a moving train crammed with passengers communicating and acting in a billion different ways and jumping on and off at a trillion different stations, some of which only appeared a matter of hours ago. Only by pausing can we observe long enough to make considered decisions that can help those who sculpt the fabric of tomorrow's society – culturally, socially, and commercially.

When I tell people that I am writing about how the internet has changed every single human on the planet, it is assumed that my book will be a dystopian vision of a painfully distorted and frightening world.

We focus a great deal on the negative impacts of the internet. The tendency to emphasize the negative rather than accentuate the positive is almost certainly due to evolutionary necessity. From our earliest beginnings, being aware of and avoiding danger has been a critical survival skill.[3] And let's be honest, a negative view has power and has been proven to be more contagious than a positive perspective.[4] "Bad news travels at the speed of light; good news travels like molasses."[5]

When you add the impact of automation to the debate, it is easy to take a personal stance, fearing for your job and envisioning mass unemployment; (the robots are coming!).

We've been spooked many times by this in our evolutionary history. Thomas Hardy's *Tess of the D'Urbervilles* is in part about the fearful change that mechanization brought to the countryside. John Maynard Keynes popularized the phrase "technological unemployment" in the 1930s, which he defined as "unemployment due to our discovery of means of economizing the use of labour outrunning the pace at which we can find new uses for labour."

John F. Kennedy created an Office of Automation and Manpower in the Department of Labor in 1961, identifying that the major domestic challenge of the 1960s was to maintain full employment at a time when automation was replacing humans.

The unknown is indeed frightening, but for me it is vital, too. The unknown can prompt the curious to investigate, and as we evolve we construct new mechanisms for survival. The opposable thumb was one such early (physical) survival mechanism. The wheel, steam power, and electricity are others.

Inventions to improve society, defence, health, and education are to be expected. Ideas to ease the burdens of life are natural.

But consider these three truths (see *Figure 1* over the page).

1. The arrival of the internet was unasked for. Necessity is often the Mother of Invention (and Dissatisfaction is

often its Father) but no social commentators, philosophers, politicians, business people, medics, or lawmakers were crying out for HTML.

2. The internet was never intended to fix something that was broken. Everything was working well in 1992. We were communicating just fine with each other. We had enjoyed global communications for a while. TAT-1 (Transatlantic No. 1) was the first transatlantic telephone cable system. It was laid between Gallanach Bay, near Oban, Scotland and Clarenville, Newfoundland between 1955 and 1956 by the cable ship Monarch. It was inaugurated on September 25, 1956, initially carrying thirty-six telephone channels. In the first twenty-four hours of public service, 588 calls were made from London to the US and 119 from London to Canada.

3. The internet did not set out to disintermediate existing social and commercial structures.[6] It was just a cool way to send documents and pictures from one computer to another; i.e., it was created in the spirit of positivity, not negativity.

It set out to be helpful, to be a facilitator.

The fact that we have learned that so many (if not all) aspects of our lives can be better facilitated is not to impugn the internet.

> **The internet has, with no agenda, upset the status quo.**

The Toronto taxi drivers who staged a mass protest against Uber on December 9 2015 might wish to ponder that it was not the internet-enabled technology that created their huge competitor, but the facilitation of a superior customer experience.

The internet discredits a previous existence where basic necessities were awkward and difficult to access and in which simple transactions were obfuscated by onerous red tape, a lack of even basic information and a strict adherence to the status quo.

This status quo recognized social strata and education, manners, and intelligence. It assumed that consumers could be unwittingly duped and that the administration of business was complicated and for experts only.

The internet is blind to all of this.

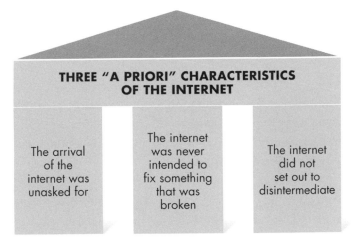

FIGURE 1: THE THREE CHARACTERISTICS OF THE INTERNET

Therefore, I don't see the internet as either good or bad. It had – and has – no agenda other than the perpetuation and growth of its own facilitation, utility, and value.

Its growth fundamentally fuels, enlarges, and reshapes a wide bandwidth of the broadest possible physiological needs from "basic" to "highly individual."

It might not be good or bad, but it does have an impact.

The impacts we create as a result of how we employ, deploy, and take advantage of the internet, automation, data, and software innovation are directly proportional to the values we each individually hold.

If we want the internet to engender, promote, or communicate terror or crime, it can. But we can also use it to widen horizons, teach, learn, and reach out, offering huge advantages to people all over the world.

The internet has increased and enhanced almost all our human capabilities. This phenomenon has created explosive change and unprecedented facilitation in a number of fundamental and unexpected ways.

And although we are all capably swimming in the internet ocean, some cannot see where they are going, others spend time drifting in strong currents, many are buffeted by wave after wave of change, and a few have a crow's nest perspective of what lies ahead.

I hope this short book adds insight and perspective.

MAN'S EXTENSIONS OF MAN

LEFT TO OUR DEVICES, WE USE OUR DEVICES

>>> "It is the persistent theme of this book that all technologies are extensions of our physical and nervous systems to increase power and speed." So wrote Marshall McLuhan in his seminal 1964 book, *Understanding Media*. (The overused word "seminal" really does apply here.)

In most of the companies I have run over the years, I have encouraged everyone – from interns to board members – to read *Understanding Media*. On every level it answers most of the difficult questions that arise concerning individuals and their relationship to current and emerging technology. Reading it informs some current personal or domestic debates; it helps companies plan competitive business strategies; and it reliably explains the development of new media, particularly those operating in the amplified and intensified space of the internet.

Understanding Media is not an easy read, and fortunately David Bobbit neatly explains McLuhan's theories.[7] McLuhan's thesis was, in essence, that the wheel extended our feet, the phone extended our voice, television extended our eyes and ears, the computer extended our brain, and electronic media, in general, extended our central nervous system.

He also recognized that the light bulb was a medium without content, whose value was to extend our spatial and temporal awareness.

In 1966, presaging in a near-visionary way the arrival of Amazon.com some thirty years later, McLuhan went on to say that, "Products will increasingly become services" because the delivery of these products through xerox copying and the telephone would change the way we access them. These electronic services would be an extension of ourselves and would meet our personalized demands.

I make this point right up front: I believe that the internet has extended man's ability to evolve at least as significantly as the opposable thumb (and later, speech) did for our ancestors.

We have now, through technology, completely outstripped our ancestors and all other animals.

David Begun, professor of anthropology at Toronto University, notes how curious it is that gorillas appear so similar to our early ancestors, while humans are so radically different (even to our recent ancestors, Neanderthal man, who became extinct only 30,000 years ago). This is despite having the same time to evolve.[8]

Add the opposable thumb and speech together – providing huge aptitude for the creation of culture – and there might be a clue.

Add the internet, and we jettison our antecedents permanently into the very dim and far distant past, as we move flat-out from making stone tools on a tiny patch of our own transitory home to being able to do almost anything, anywhere on the planet, at the same time as everyone else. Homo sapiens has upgraded itself to Homo omnipotens (see *Figure 2*).

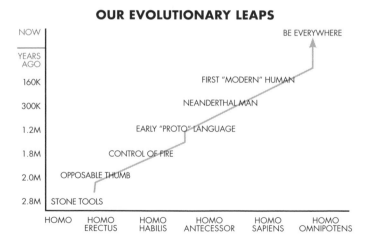

OUR EVOLUTIONARY LEAPS

FIGURE 2: EVOLUTIONARY LEAPS IN HUMAN DEVELOPMENT

Sigmund Freud, in *Civilization and its Discontents*, assesses what technology has done to the human being, making him into a kind of god with artificial limbs, a prosthetic god. "When he puts on all his auxiliary organs, he is truly magnificent," Freud writes, "but those organs have not grown onto him and they still give him much trouble at times."[9]

> The internet makes us "omnipotent". We are not Gods. But our forefathers might see us as "godlike".

The things we can do today would indeed seem "godlike," or certainly omnipotent, to our recent forefathers. But, in fact, Freud did not see the internet and we *have* grown into them. The phone is now an amplified hand incorporating a secondary, more powerful brain, a seemingly infinite-reaching set of digits, and eyes that can see around the planet and look at multiple places at the same time.

What is really driving this "technological opposable thumb" today is the harnessing of four forces: data, automation, new technologies, and the internet. I call this DANTI.[10]

Together these four influences pump more and more power into our devices and therefore give us more capabilities (see *Figure 3* over the page).

DANTI. OUR NEW OMNIPOTENT BODY PART
AND EXTENSION OF OURSELVES

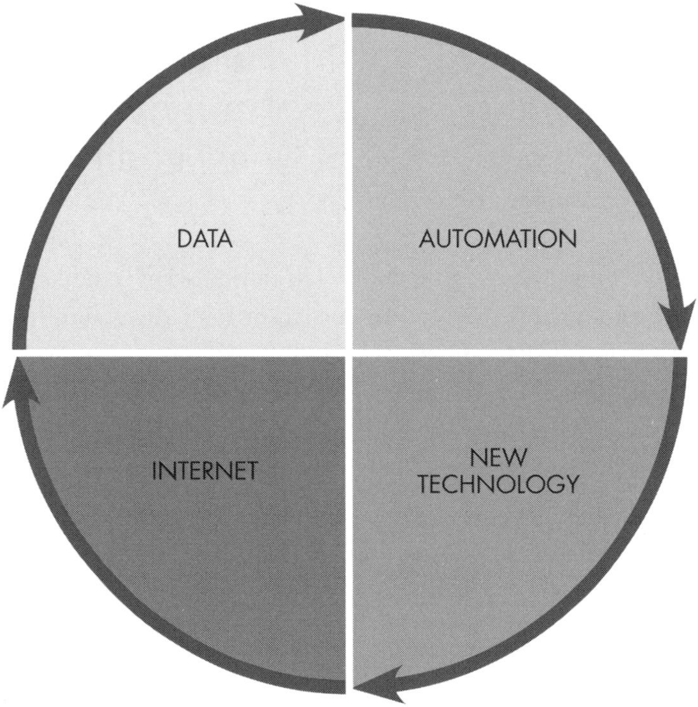

FIGURE 3: THE FOUR FORCES WORKING TOGETHER
TO EXTEND AND EXPAND OUR CAPABILITIES

Today, the modernizing elements of DANTI drive our activities daily and bring to fruition another of McLuhan's earliest theses. He posited that, "Rapidly, we approach the final phase of the extension of man – the technological simulation of consciousness, when the creative process of knowing will be collectively and corporately extended to the whole of human society, much as we have already extended our senses and nerves by the various media."

The whole of human society is indeed undergoing a "sensory big bang". No corner of our lives remains unaffected.

History now tells us that when Tim Berners-Lee put up the first-ever website on August 6 1991, it was merely the aperitivo. What was served up next has been truly extraordinary.

WE KNOW

 In fact, we now know that part one of the internet is well and truly over.[11]

Internet development has moved silently and progressively, first capturing military and industrial use, then commercial advantage and, of course, now social dependence, individual independence, and societal interdependence.

We now have "part two" (or to keep the metaphor running, the *antipasto*). And we know that there is so much more to come. In quality and size, the next course is surely going to be a giant leap.

We have become accustomed to huge numbers and exponential change.

The technology that brings us the internet has developed at a dizzying rate. We now live in the zettabyte age. One zettabyte, a measure of the sheer capacity of information the internet can hold, is 1,000,000,000,000,000,000,000 bytes, or 250 billion full-length HD movies on DVD. As I have been writing this book, the forecast for internet capacity has been steadily growing, and it is projected that by the close of 2015, internet traffic will exceed 1 zettabyte and will double by 2019.[12] The amount of electronic information already stored is calculated to be approximately 3.0 zettabytes.

In this zettabyte explosion, video is predicted to be the main agent of growth. We like video. Video is easy to assimilate. Video works easily in different languages. It's a shorthand that can explain things effortlessly when done well. It's the reason the number of people watching YouTube each day increased by 40% between March 2014 and April 2015[13] and it's the reason why YouTube's global "watch time" is up 60% year-over-year, with mobile watch time more than double from what it was a year ago.[14]

> The internet is the biggest thing we humans have ever created. And it always will be.

The simple fact is that the internet is the biggest thing we have ever created on this planet. Bigger than any physical structure, bigger than any geography. And it keeps growing.[15]

By 2020, the digital universe will contain more digital bits than there are stars in the actual universe.[16]

So, yes, let's agree: it's ginormous.

But here's the thing.

We know.

We know about huge valuations for small start-ups (Oculus Rift, $2 billion). We know about massive customer bases (Facebook had, by end of 2015, 1.49 billion users). We know about (what the experts call) disintermediation; we know we are watching TV in a completely new and liberated way. We know how to use and abuse the internet. We know how to get what we want.

We know so much about the facilitation of the internet because we are living inside it. All the time. Living inside the interent with Freud's omnipotent "artificial limbs" at our disposal we have changed as a species. We have become significantly upgraded versions of the human model of just fifteen years ago.

SO WHAT DOES IT ALL MEAN?

 Part two of the internet has enabled us to know and do more things than our very immediate 20th century ancestors. By that, I mean my mum and dad.

It is more than a physical tool, because it has become a physiological necessity and has consequently moved beyond industrial, commercial, and social usage to the new and powerful realm of the special and the personal.

"Special and Personal" is a powerful realm because our deep physiological need for the internet has now shaped our physical, psychological, and emotional actions and behaviour, making us all more capable and more individual at the same time.

We are significantly upgraded versions of the human model of just fifteen years ago.

We now actively mould its capabilities to our own view of what's important and valuable – and what isn't. Each of us has become a more individual entity. Consider this: no two people have the same collection of mobile apps.[17] The technology has morphed to our individual DNA, and activates and enhances our daily actions in a totally exclusive way.

THE IMPACT OF THE INTERNET IS HYPER-EVOLUTIONARY

>>

The internet is so fundamental that it is now at "Priority Level One" on most countries' National Security Strategic Agendas[18] and its absence has been forecast to set economies back more than thirty years with critical disruptions, mass unemployment, and devastating crime.

But principally it remains the highest priority for us because of the opportunities it offers.

These opportunities affect us all. Whether they benefit us all is not the point. Some will, some won't, because it is not the role of the internet to bestow goodness on all and sundry. It just exists, i.e., it is a physiological need that some of us choose to expand and others choose to minimize.

For the voyeur and super-secretive, it adds levels of usability never before imagined. For the broadcaster, blogger,

vlogger (video blogger), and myriad fundraising social en-
terprises, it is a dream come true. Inherently the internet
has no "view". But to "readjust" Melvin Kranzberg's First
Law of Technology, neither is the internet neutral–because
it does have an impact.[19]

The impact (special and personal) offers highly prized
opportunities for high-ticket items (smart watches, virtual reality experiences, space travel, gaming, elaborate
smart-wear) and alters the way we fundamentally behave
in private and public. In fact, the habit-forming routines
and context-dependent repetitive actions that create the
regular patterns of our daily existence have been reshaped
by internet-reliant technology in a fundamental way. We
have evolved and now operate, quite naturally, in a highly
sophisticated way.

WE ARE ALL INTELLIGENT OBJECTS

>> Sleeping, waking, eating, conversing, entertaining, shopping, dating, learning, celebrating, playing, and relaxing have all become altered states due to the invasive and immersive impact of the internet. In fact, every personal human undertaking is now connected by the internet and interconnected to any person, any company, and any organization we choose. Sometimes – often, in fact – we don't realize we are choosing to be connected, so subtle and fluid and free is the way we now like to live.

In fact, some of the dreary aspects of our lives are automated in the background, and solutions are served up like the arrival of an invisible, magical personal butler. Think about checking in at an airport and compare it to ten years ago.

Electricity, the automobile, the airplane and TV have caused seismic shifts in our more recent history, but the internet has gone further, affecting and changing all parts of our lives, including, of course, electricity, the automobile, the airplane, and TV! We now have internet-automated electricity (Nest and Hive, for example), internet-enabled driverless cars, internet-aided airplane travel, and disintermediated TV.

The internet has created new agendas within the regular pattern of our lives because it has given us all equal access (and all at the same time) to a transformative technology that re-evaluates our lives and adds value simultaneously. As we go about our daily business, we mainly see it as a beneficial force, and we are increasingly more attracted to it and at its service.

Sleep used to be a time where nothing would happen, to ensure alertness the next day. We were awakened from sleep by an alarm clock, which was for many people a timely reminder of the intrusion of a socio-economic time discipline into their sleep cycle. (Prior to alarm clocks, the sun did the trick and night closed the day.)

Sleep is now something we do between checking our smartphones. We want, indeed we programme, our sleep cycle to be interrupted by messaging and updates. Sleep is not so much a period of rest as a pause in our online connectivity.

Reading a chapter of a book was once a mentally intimate activity. Now reading is aided or interrupted by external digital aids, assistants and updates (see *Figure 4*).

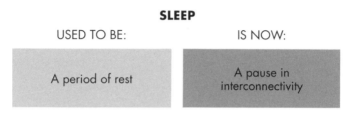

SLEEP

USED TO BE:	IS NOW:
A period of rest	A pause in interconnectivity

FIGURE 4: THE INTERNET HAS CHANGED NEARLY EVERY ASPECT OF OUR LIVES, INCLUDING SLEEP

Now reading and sleeping are both essentially the same thing. They are both intervals of time of varying length between checking the status of our – and other's – interconnectivity. Many people sleep with a specific application of connectivity, by using their internet-enabled devices to monitor sleep patterns, set an alarm for an appropriately rested period, and even donate processing power to a worthy cause while their device is not 100% dedicated to themselves.[20] All three of these sleep functions are active agents in an improved life.

Our relationship to food and eating has changed, too. Home delivery, restaurant searches, menu suitability, table bookings, diet management, and cooking have all been elevated to a high-level skill set. The humdrum ritual and regularity of eating has now been converted to part-humdrum, part-entertainment, and part-electronic processing.

Nutrition Research and Practice[21] examined lifestyle patterns and dietary behaviour based on the level of internet addiction of Korean adolescents. Data were collected from 853 Korean junior high school students.[22]

The study demonstrated that there were "high-risk" internet users. This group ate smaller meals, had less of an appetite, skipped meals, and snacked more than their "potential-risk" and "normal-risk" internet-user counterparts. Moreover, the diet quality of high-risk internet users was poorer than that of potential-risk internet users and normal-risk internet users.

More bytes equalled less bites (see *Figure 5*).

FIGURE 5: THOSE AT HIGH RISK FOR INTERNET ADDICTION ATE LESS, ATE SMALLER MEALS, SKIPPED MEALS, AND SNACKED MORE THAN THEIR COUNTERPARTS NOT AT HIGH RISK

Bite-size menu options are a hot new thing at casual chain restaurants like California Pizza Kitchen and Houlihan's. Of course, small plates are a concession to budget-conscious eaters and possibly an attempt at a more upscale feel. But in a surprising twist, Bob Hartnett, CEO of Houlihan's, claims that the change is specially targeted at younger, web-savvy customers. Small plates, he explains, are for diners who are "just as comfortable sharing a plate of food as they are sharing social media."[23]

Being "on top of the food chain" was an important evolutionary step for humans. It was only 400,000 years ago that man began to hunt in packs on a regular basis. And 300,000 years ago, the domestication of fire allowed us to start cooking our food, enabling us to eat a wider variety of foods with less health hazards. It has even been argued that cooked foods helped Homo sapiens develop larger brains.[24]

It is not impossible to suggest that the internet is now re-addressing our relationship to food and reframing it in the context of "byte-sized information" and the formalization of "sharing".

Eating as a direct function of internet behaviour is now related to technology. Its role in our evolutionary development will diminish somewhat as the importance of increased internet activity gathers pace.

Looking at the growth of "the quantified self" can provide evidence for this. We can now record, store, and analyze our food intake as data using our smartphones and watches, or the personalized Nike Fuelband. We can measure carbohydrates, fats, and alcohol (and much more) and measure them against our exercise regimens and health ordinances.

Travel is now a finger-clicking exercise with precision timing. Delays and lack of information are increasingly being replaced by instant access to information and by transport methods that flow more beneficially, due to much improved management information.

Automotive manufacturers, for example, recognize the value of including smart navigation, even at the lower end of their range. They are linking cars to the internet, as well as to satellites, to provide micro details of journeys. The data is useful for drivers and essential for manufacturers. This explains why a group of German automakers agreed to pay slightly more than €2.5 billion ($2.7 billion) for Nokia's digital mapping service, Here,[25] prevailing over Silicon Valley bidders in a battle for a key enabling technology for self-driving cars.

Cars are no longer just "self-propelled passenger vehicles that usually have four wheels and an internal combustion engine."[26] Now they are intelligent objects, wired into the same networks as you and me and every other object on the planet.

The mode of travel we choose depends on the time, distance, speed, cost, and comfort factors that can now be very quickly assessed. Once we are traveling, real-time uploading and downloading of location status into the network is simply second nature.

Formal and informal conversations have changed. They can embrace a huge bandwidth of instant content. This can happen physically or digitally or both at the same time. Debates can flare up in an instant, spontaneously backed up by huge data. Opinions can be changed and long-held beliefs can be fundamentally altered with instantaneous reference to any of the thirty million articles on Wikipedia. "Let's Google it" has turned the giant search company into a verb as natural-sounding to us as "Let's look it up." We each have access to the online "elder" who answers, corroborates, and notifies the instant we make contact.

> Now we can communicate, even when we are not communicating.

Conversation could once be defined as chat, comment, debate, or discussion. It has been one of the most vital forms of human-to-human connectivity. Now conversation has expanded to become a formidable skill set. We can intelligently converse with more than one person at the same time. We can converse at no cost over the longest distances and talk face-to-face with each other.[27] As we shall see later, we can communicate even when we are not communicating, by offering data and profile preferences to a networked society, which eventually responds to us in a meaningful reply to our data donation.

The pursuit of leisure is at our fingertips. Control of the packaged vacation is no longer just in the hands of a few travel agents. The internet has made agents of us all. Airbnb has swept across the globe at an alarming rate, facilitating peer-to-peer accommodation booking. The complexity of travel has been demystified as self-booking has become second nature.

Airbnb and the taxi company Uber succeed by "reverse networking."[28] Once taxicabs were a network – a yellow one in New York or a black one in London, for example – and fares were individual people. Now we are upgraded to the status of a "network" and the cabs are the individuals hoping to attract and access us.[29]

THE "HOLODECK" IS A STEP CLOSER

Mark Zuckerberg might have had McLuhan's "technological simulation of consciousness" in mind when his company, Facebook, bought Oculus Rift on July 22 2014 for $400m in cash, plus 23.1m Facebook shares. The whole deal was almost an astonishing $2 billion, because the owners of Oculus will receive a further $300m in incentives if the technology hits certain "milestones" in the future. At the time, the deal looked astonishing, because the technology was in its infancy when Facebook bought it and did not intersect neatly with the internet.

One wonders what these "milestones" might be. Oculus Rift is a virtual reality head-mounted display. It is hardware. It has competitors, such as Microsoft's HoloLens, HTC's Vive, Sony's Project Morpheus, and Samsung's Gear. Virtual reality is also known as "immersive media" and is, in essence, computer-simulated "real life."

It is a very real, altered state.

Virtual reality technology and experimentation easily pre-dates the internet. Although the term can be traced back to Monsieur Antonin Artaud in 1938,[30] it was an American polymath (a "computer philosopher" writer, computer scientist, film director, and composer of classical music) named Jaron Zepel Lanier who in 1985 founded the modern business we know as virtual reality.

Virtual reality is the stuff of *Star Trek*, and its centre of gravity has for a long time lain in the lap of super-geeks who have marvelled at, toyed with, and experimented in the possibilities of the technology.

In many respects, it has taken a while for this technology to begin to intersect with the internet, but now that it has, the *Star Trek* dream of being able to holiday on the "Holodeck" is looking a step nearer. The Holodeck is regularly used by the crew of the Starship Enterprise to recreate places that remind them of home or are familiar Earth-bound settings. The crew can also participate in interactive stories, and practice a wide range of recreation, sports, and skills.

SCREENS THAT "HIDE" AND "SEEK"

>> Virtual reality, augmented reality and 3D are as much an extension of man as the wheel, the phone, the TV, and the computer. Through a screen they take us into a different, expanded, and enhanced place; a place that does not conform to the physics of terrestrial Earth.

The author C.S. Lewis, I conjecture, may have read Artaud's book as he began to construct a fantasy just a step away from ordinary life. The eponymous wardrobe in *The Lion, The Witch and The Wardobe* is a doorway into an alternative reality. The wardrobe acts like a modern-day screen.

The word "screen" has two meanings. It is both something you look at and, of course, something that hides you. Screens have always been used as a partition to keep certain activities out of the sight of others. They could contain an intimate and personal world.

We use screens to access both meanings. We look into them to activate our lives by seeking new opportunities, and we go behind them to hide, protect, create, or enhance other important versions of our lives, many of which are private.

Those of us with a smartphone, tablet, or laptop unanimously approve of our screen lives, and we have become a common generational type.

Child, teenager, baby boomer, yuppie, generations X and Y, millennial, hipster – all these conform to cultural stereotypes.

We are all screenagers.[31]

We are all the same cultural stereotype. We are all Screenagers.

A study by Kleiner Perkins Caufield and Byers found that average users check their phone up to 150 times a day. In its annual "Internet Trends" report, the firm digs deep into smartphone behaviours and found that people check their phones, on average, 23 times a day for messaging, 22 times for voice calls, and 18 times to get the time.[32] This leaves the remaining screen time for our everyday promiscuous, random, and often vicarious viewing.

We take our screens with us everywhere, peering into them, interacting with them, and briefing them to execute certain commands.

We cannot put them down. They cannot leave our hands. We walk and talk and text and check apps all at the same time. They augment the sensory parts of our behaviour – sight, sound, and touch.

A March 2013 survey revealed that three quarters of people use their mobile phones while sitting on the toilet.[33]

The poll of 2,000 people, conducted by Sony and O2, also revealed that a quarter of men choose to sit on the toilet basin rather than stand, just so that their hands are free to use their mobiles.

While 59% of men and women admitted to sending texts and 45% to sending emails, nearly a third said they have taken a call and 24% revealed that they have phoned someone while on the toilet.

The poll revealed that most people use their phones on the toilet simply because they have nothing better to do.

And 29% said it was because they "wanted to prevent boredom setting in" and 12% said that they felt pressure to stay on top of emails and messages, even while in the bathroom.

The phone companies are creating a "water-resistant" handset after surveys showed that 15% of people admitted to having dropped their mobile down the toilet.

The commands we give our screens and the notifications we receive are not confined to just our own physical space, awareness, and ability. They are automated.

But automation is not a system in a vacuum, operating independently of the outside world. It is the result of our own inputs. We pull the levers and press the buttons that activate automation in a 21st century version of the Jacquard Loom, first demonstrated in 1801.

This highly automated loom was controlled by a "chain of cards," a number of punched cards laced together into a continuous sequence. Multiple rows of holes were punched on each card, with one complete card corresponding to one row of the design.

We screenagers do the same as we enter data into a world behind the screen, both seeking and secreting the things we need and desire. Our data inputs create the design for our lives, composing an intricate design of desires, requirements, rejections, and mundane transactions.

What we are punching on our mobile screens are built-in and bought-in apps. Apps augment everything we do: shopping, relaxing, seeking, playing – you name it, there's an app for it.

APP-MAN

 Apps exploded onto the scene on July 10 2008 via an update to iTunes. The first ones were games (such as Super Monkey Ball, Enigmo, and At Bat) but eBay was there, too, as a pioneer of mobile-based shopping.

In just seven years there are now more than 2,141,957 apps available on all types of devices.[34]

We have taken this augmentation to our lives like fish to water. The speed of the development (and inclusion into our everyday lives) of app-activated services has been astonishing. But it is not the speed that is the most curious part of this particular outbreak of electronic human activation activity.

It is how we use them.

There is one part of our personal world that we choose to privately inhabit that is sacrosanct and super-secret. This world is rarely open to friends or relatives, or, even, progeny. So protected is this world that highly complex encryption software is deployed to keep its contents safe. Often this world will not be shared even with a spouse.

It is the world of personal finance.

We have accepted that personal financial management through apps is a normal part of our lives. These are testament to the way we use apps effortlessly and with a casualness that belies the impact they can have on our lives.

Rudimentary mobile banking was conducted through SMS in the 1990s, but it was the Norwegian bank, Fokus Bank that, in September 1999, detonated, through WAP,[35] the whole mobile banking explosion that now is such a fundamental part of our lives.

Now most major banks have a mobile app, allowing us to make fairly complicated financial transactions very easily at the tap of a finger.

Retail banking has undergone a dramatic transformation in a very short number of years. Not new to the benefits of technology, banks introduced automated bank tellers–ATMs–in the mid-1960s. The introduction of the ATM marked not just the dawn of contemporary digital banking, but also the beginning of large-scale automation across the banking sector, which has led to a decline in physical bank branches and, of course, physical bank tellers.

Personal finance has never been more personal with online and app development coming faster and faster.

Atom Bank, a new UK entrant in financial services, neatly brings together the rise in mobile personal banking and the rise of virtual and augmented technology. Customers will be able to open accounts and carry out all their banking activity only from their smartphones.

The 2014 start-up said it wants to, "Set new standards for the banking sector" when it comes to technology. The company plans to use 3D visualizations and gaming technology for its app, and plans to integrate cutting-edge biometric security.

Augmented banking is heading McLuhan's way. Soon banking will be an extension of ourselves, allowing us to simply transfer and receive money through cyberspace in a way that will feel like we are actually touching and seeing the money.

Financial transactions are not, of course, about moving real money around.

Money is three things – and none of these are "real". Money is a store of "value", which means people can save it and use it later, making purchases over time. It is a "unit of account", that is, it provides a common base for prices. And it is a "medium of exchange", something that people can use to buy and sell from one another.

We have a "monetary system" rather than a fixed amount of money, and for a long time this system fixed the unit of account to gold. Most nations abandoned the gold standard as the basis of their monetary systems at some point in the 20th century (although many hold substantial gold reserves).

In April 2015, Citibank's global chief economist, Willem Buiter, announced[36] that cash should be wiped out and purely digital currency used. There are many high-profile supporters of this, including Ken Rogoff, professor of public policy and professor of economics at Harvard University, and Bill Gates. They both argue that a purely digital economy allows for great flexibility and increased security.

We are looking at a future where money will no longer be physical, tangible, or "real". It will become a series of transactions in the virtual world of cyberspace. It will become a virtual handshake – an electronic extension of our own personal worth.

It was against this background that Bitcoin exploded onto the scene, and to say its impact has been seismic would be an understatement. Bitcoin's inventor (or inventors, no one is quite sure), Satoshi Nakamoto, published the invention on October 31 2008 in a research paper called, "Bitcoin:

A Peer-to-Peer Electronic Cash System."[37] Nakamoto wrote: "A purely peer-to-peer version of electronic cash would allow online payments to be sent directly from one party to another without going through a financial institution."

Bitcoin requires some explanation and I quote from Marc Bevand's blog, which spells out how it works quite clearly.[38] "Bitcoin is the *world's first invention of a decentralized electronic currency*, with no central authority or trusted parties whatsoever, as its inventor originally describes. Not even the Bitcoin developers themselves have special control of Bitcoin."

Bevand explains in more detail:

- "Bitcoin is like *digital gold*.

- By design, there is a known, immutable, fixed supply of Bitcoins, similar to gold being available in limited quantity on Earth. There are 2.1 quadrillion indivisible units of value (0.00000001 Bitcoins), and not one more will ever exist.

- Bitcoins are digital; therefore you can *instantly transfer* them to anybody across the world.

- Bitcoins are *stored locally* on your electronic device (cell phone, computer), contrary to being stored in an account managed by a financial institution. This is similar to how you can store cash or gold in a physical location of your choice. This means there is no "Bitcoin account" that can be frozen by someone in power (e.g., your spouse making malicious claims to seize a bank account during a divorce).

- Bitcoin transactions are *technically irreversible*. There is no mechanism to revert a transaction, other than convincing the recipient to send the Bitcoins back. This solves the fraud problem for merchants, as all payments they receive are final, whether fraudulent or not. (On the downside, like cash or gold, if Bitcoins are stolen from you, the chance of recovering them is generally slim.)

- Payments are sent directly from one party to another *without going through a financial institution*, similar to how cash or gold can be handed directly to someone. You do so by sending them from your computer to the recipient's computer through the Bitcoin network (which is nothing more than other computers running Bitcoin). Since no one can realistically prevent a computer from getting internet access one way or another, no one can regulate or block transactions (e.g., oppressive governments financially repressing activists).

- Finally, there is no financial institution, bank, or company operating Bitcoin, just like there is no company in charge of operating "gold." There is no internet server to shut down or to terminate Bitcoin. It exists merely as an application running on your computer, which communicates with other Bitcoin users over the internet. The Bitcoin network is called a peer-to-peer network, and this design makes it effectively *indestructible*, as long as the medium of communication (internet) exists."[39]

Bitcoin's open-source software was released in 2009. Within less than six years it is rewriting the six-hundred-year rationale of how we use our money, a rationale that had not really changed since the birth of modern banking in 14th century Florence.

Bitcoin is a genuine extension of man's "worth", because what you see is what you get, unmediated, moderated, or managed in any way.

Bitcoin is managed and operated on a public ledger that records Bitcoin transactions, called Blockchain. Blockchain is in its infancy as I write this book, but within twelve months of its publication I can safely assert that it will be driving entirely new agendas on the internet.

Blockchain upgrades the world wide web and gives us a new transformative protocol.

Blockchain is today what Tim Berners-Lee's invention of the World Wide Web was back in 1989. It is an entirely new internet protocol. In early 2015, both IBM and Nasdaq began experimenting with Blockchain to extend its usage beyond Bitcoin, utilizing its huge ledger management system to empower, among other things, the Internet of Things.

We wait to see the full impact of this technological tsunami, but there is absolutely no doubt it will be transformative and, in developmental terms, life changing.

A more straightforward peer-to-peer product is WeSwap,[40] founded in 2010 by Jared Jesner and Simon Sacerdoti.

WeSwap.com provides an online person-to-person currency exchange service. It matches people who are travelling in opposite directions from each other with the currency they need and automatically swaps their money without using banks or retail outlets. WeSwap allows customers to instantly spend or withdraw their money by using its multi-currency prepaid MasterCard, holding up to twelve different currencies. It serves holidaymakers, expats, and business travellers around the world.

WeSwap's message is that it's simple, secure, and means everyone gets a better deal on travel money. Jesner and Sacerdoti call it social currency, and they claim the service can save customers serious money. "While an airport bureau de change can charge 13%-17% above the interbank rate, we charge just 1%," they say.[41]

Unlike the truly pioneering Bitcoin, existing financial institutions are not excluded. But the conventional currency exchange system is bypassed. WeSwap is just one example of the rise in peer-to-peer financial technology products, of which there are many.

But they are also an example of a significant cultural shift in our general behaviour and attitude.[42]

This is neatly summarized by Daniel Eberhard, the founder of Koho, a Canadian-driven banking technology platform. He says, "Millennial consumers have increasingly higher expectations from the products they interact with. Banks simply aren't designed to keep pace with innovation. Every time a tech company bites off a portion of the banking eco-system, it's because they're meeting customer expectations better than banks can."

The way we count, use, spend, and transmit money is changing for the first time. We are now a species that can develop financially without any exchange of tangible assets.

New thinking, new business, new politics, new relation-ships, new selling, new buying, new leisure, and new transport – all these add up to a global and generic human skills upgrade.

This skills upgrade has two main drivers.

SKILLS TRANSFERENCE AND SKILLS EXPANSION

Skills transference, is a process by which all our regular interactions with business and politics are reversed (see *Figure 6*).

Skills expansion, is an enhanced practice whereby all our relationships with vendors are professionalized. Skills expansion has taught individuals to regularly deploy a range of skills that would normally be in the domain of businesses, or even academia and politics.

SKILLS TRANSFERENCE

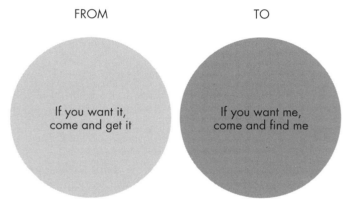

FIGURE 6: SKILLS TRANSFERENCE AFFECTS AND ENHANCES
ATTITUDE, LANGUAGE, BEHAVIOUR, AND EXPECTATION

SKILLS
TRANSFERENCE

 Skills transference affects and enhances attitude, language, behaviour, and expectation. And it operates in the reverse network system of access and attraction.

Business used to be a commercial network within which we were required to operate the buying and selling of our goods and services. Now we are the network, an agile data network, into which individual businesses must pitch their offerings.

Businesses must strive to gain access to us. The successful ones do this by following and responding to our individual data. The clever ones do this by recognizing that customers are no different than them. They will actively bring the customer into the heart of the company, often crowdsourcing ideas or instantly responding to individual feedback.

We now do not take businesses at face value. We put them on constant notice. *We* communicate to *them*. We sell ourselves, through our explicit donation of our data.

We use words like "personal data" and "profile" instead of "private information". We "click to accept" instead of saying "yes". We "transact" with vendors as much as we "go shopping". While most of us probably don't operate personal "KPIs"[43], we are practiced in the art of understanding vendor standards and demand high levels of service and quality. We use peer-to-peer mean scores to calibrate our evaluations.

There is an irony in this language and behavioural transference. Many businesses are being encouraged to communicate in a more personal or "human" way.[44] So in an unexpected turn of events, ordinary people are adopting business behaviours and businesses are adopting ordinary human behaviour!

This had led to an emergence of H2H communications (human to human) in favour of B2C (business to consumer or B2B (business to business).

But I believe this transference, in the "reverse network", has led to something deeper. Now that we have the expertise to trade more beneficially, the relationship is more C2B, that is to say, consumer to business. Consumers are sending the messages for business to react to.

> ## We can "see it", want it and get it in seconds. Speed of delivery is our "KPI"

We input our data into businesses. We don't necessarily want a nice human interaction in response, but we do want delivery times met and quality standards obeyed.

We have become so business-like as individuals that marketers need to ditch the processes of B2C communication and begin to adopt and adapt the rules of C2B when talking to consumers.

This form of communication is about logic, information, reassurance, experience, and knowledge.

We behave as businesses do by using (albeit rudimentary) buying strategies to get costs down. We evaluate items against each other. We are confident in contacting the right people to complain and renegotiate what we think was a bad deal.

We are becoming more and more accustomed to an "I see it, I want it, now" mentality whereby too-long delivery times can mean a cancelled order.

We have, in fact, higher and higher expectations of quality and delivery. And we expect our businesses and, indeed, our politicians, to stick to their agreements or explain clearly why they are changing their policies (see *Figure 7*).

"CONSUMER TO BUSINESS" SKILLS MEANS CUSTOMERS HAVE MASSIVELY INCREASED THEIR POWER OF COMMAND

I will compare,
analyze, negotiate.
I will judge you by my
own performance targets.
Your standards must match mine
or I will fire you. After this,
I might give you my data.

I will buy
something
from you

FIGURE 7: BUSINESSES ARE TRANSFORMING THEIR APPROACH
TO A CONSUMER-TO-BUSINESS MODEL OF COMMUNICATION

SKILLS TRANSFERENCE IS MAKING LIFE UNPREDICTABLE

 Today there are few conventional barriers between work, life, business, customer, politician, and voter. The 2014 independence vote in Scotland was as much an outpouring of ordinary views from "the man in the street" as it was "informed views" of both politicians and journalists. "Mood" and "point of view" are now as powerful as the doctrinaire socioeconomic divisions of "working class" or "democrat" or "Euro-sceptic." Such moods and views are garnered successfully by, for example, 38degree.org, an organization that actively canvasses and collects opinions and transforms them into political power. This demonstrates skills transference of enormous potential.

The 2015 UK general election demonstrated that the data used by pollsters was no match for the individually donated data at the ballot box. We have become used to privately ticking boxes with our preferences on the privacy of our own screens. We can easily hold more than one personality trait as we skip from Facebook to LinkedIn. Hence it was no surprise that only the exit poll proved accurate. Dipstick polling in the conventional manner was less accurate. Politics is no longer a framework within which we make our choices. We are the framework and politicians have to win us over, one by one. Pollsters have to recognize the growing strength of our individuality and the unpredictability that brings. The electorate is a cohesive network of individuals that politicians have to attract and access.

SKILLS
EXPANSION

 We have expanded our daily personal lives in the workplace more than ever, and in real time. We check personal e-mails in a coexistent way with business emails. We "chat" with family and loved ones while attending business meetings. There are many similar examples, but the one that immediately typifies this blurring of "work life" and "personal life" is the use of personal headphones. As the rise of an open plan grew, so did the rise of personal headsets to delineate "personal space" and emit a "please do not disturb" notice. One of many blogs commenting on this phenomenon[45] outlines five major benefits of being in your private "headspace" at work:

1. **It sets expectations that you are occupied.** When wearing headphones, you project an expectation that you are working or engrossed in deep thought. People are less inclined to interrupt you.

2. **Headphones create your own work zone.** If you work in a noisy or busy environment, putting on headphones can be the ticket to your own private "in the zone" space to tune in to your music and turn off the office chaos soundtrack.

3. **It helps you motivate. Music can be a great motivator.** In addition to isolating you, music can serve to pump up your energy and mood. Keep your inspirational music close at hand. What's your power song?

4. **Wearing headphones prevents distractions and interruptions.** When you are concentrating on a tough task, the last thing you want is to be distracted by the latest hallway chat about politics or sports scores. Let music eliminate distractions and keep you on task.

5. **It lets you choose your own attitude.** Whether your attitude needs a quick pickup or even a few minutes of calm, let music set your mood. Several minutes of peaceful music can be a great break from the hustle and bustle of the day.

The simple act of wearing headphones at work is a symbolic, outward sign of our changed and expanded personalities. We are operating in one world–our own individual world–and we access everyone else's world through technology by switching ourselves in and out.

Our human upgrade gives us access to everyone else's world – at the flick of a mental switch.

Politicians need to understand that this skills expansion has come at the expense of political dogma and speech-making. That is because we can now know and see almost everything they are doing. Lies can be verified. We can all view the YouTube "side-by-side" videos demonstrating both promises and broken promises. We can put ourselves, instantly, into the politician's world.

We are now fitted with McLuhan's final extension—the technological simulation of consciousness. We are extended into, and can see, the whole of human society.

Homo sapiens is reshaping into Homo omnipotens. With the internet at the core of what we do, think, and say, we are spreading ourselves ever wider, extending our capabilities faster than in any previous generation. And we are spreading ourselves across more forms and functions of the modern world than ever conceived possible.

TRAVEL BROADENS THE BODY

HOMO OMNIPOTENS CAN GO WHEREVER AND WHENEVER WE WANT.

>> We travel in ways we have never traveled before. At one time, travel was a journey between two points. Today, travel is an experiential trip to multiple places at multiple times and in many different time zones. And because of the exciting intermediate points that we discover during the travel process (for instance, we chance upon an interesting artist while looking for a holiday) the entire experience can be ramified at each such point, providing a multiplexed, multivariate experience.

In traveling, we travel more.

We can take ourselves to wherever we want to go, look around, and converse with locals without ever leaving home, and at no more extra cost than our normal living expenses.

We can hear local languages, retrieve recipes for exotic dishes, look at places in real time or from a historical perspective, and talk to people anywhere on the planet over messaging systems, voice, or video.

We can research the history of where we are going, down to specific places and people. We can discover the lineage of people we are meeting. We can look at local legislation and uncover local news stories.

Obviously we can check the weather, but we can also check the minutiae of the weather, down to the exact hour of our arrival. We can verify the weather data through live webcams, adding unquestionable visual assurance to the raw data of information. We can even see what people are wearing in various locales, and if their umbrellas are up.

We can take a dip into the deep, perhaps less obvious, cultural layers of a country. We can immerse ourselves in a way our ancestors never were able. They merely skimmed the surface, whereas we can lift the lid on the remotest of places and, with practiced ease, explore and sample as much or as little as we like.

> The world can be cupped in our hands and traveled through our fingers.

Our keyboards are not just for typing words – they are now our maps. Our fingers are curious cursors, combining together to quench a ten-digit thirst for information. This information appears after we have made our digital input requests and is happy to be hard at work in both our waking and sleeping hours.

These "travel agents" charge no commission and offer a bespoke service.

GETTING USED TO OUR NEW PROSTHESIS –THE PHONE

We can also travel physically in a completely transformative way, with expensive guidance systems and the fullest possible knowledge of estimated arrival times, local resources, and areas of special interest.

Traveling with smartphones is absolutely obligatory. These devices have become indispensable parts of our daily operations – yes, indispensable parts of our bodies.

Indispensable, yes, but also still new and hazardous at times. How often have we bumped into people or objects while scrutinising our smartphones? How often have we sneaked a peek at our smartphone while driving–even though we know it's dangerous, even illegal.

A recent study from the National Safety Council found that 26% of all car accidents were caused by a driver using a cell phone, but remarkably attributed only 5% to texting while driving.[46]

Ohio State University has conducted research in this area.[47] More than 1,500 pedestrians were estimated to be treated in emergency rooms in 2010 for injuries related to using a cell phone while walking, according to a nationwide study. The number of such injuries has more than doubled since 2005, even though the total number of pedestrian injuries dropped during that time. And researchers believe that the actual number of injured pedestrians is actually much higher than these results suggest.

In Chongqing, China, city authorities have designated a 100-foot "cell phone lane" for people using their phones while walking. "First mobile phone sidewalks in China," declares a notice next to it.

This may well be a stunt similar to that in Washington, DC, in July 2014 and the e-lane for pedestrians in Philadelphia (actually an April Fool's joke). It is most likely that these initiatives were aimed to bring the dangers of walking while on smartphones to the public's attention.

But they are an emerging sign of the different ways in which we now walk. Due to smartphone internet technology, we are changing the way we commune with each other and the way city authorities develop public health and safety codes. In many respects, these issues were addressed by Apple with the arrival of the Apple Watch, which weaves the prosthetic phone more naturally to our bodies, almost becoming part of our skin.

Wrapping technology around our skin has been an exciting enhancement ever since 1910, when Cadillac became the first company to offer a passenger car with a fully enclosed cabin, a major change from the vehicles of the time.[48]

Today we can be connected on the road through on-board wifi, global navigation satellites, and touchscreen information centres with real-time TV, news, and weather. We can choose to have radar-assisted braking, traffic sign recognition, and sensors that track road markings to keep you in your lane. Infrared systems are now available to detect pedestrians at night. These display a black-and-white view of the road ahead, displaying any potential hazards in red and even auto-flashing the headlights to alert anyone who might have stepped into the street without looking.[49]

When you slide into your new automobile in 2015, you are sitting in a car that has more computing power than the system used to guide the Apollo astronauts to the moon.

And the technology and the zettabytes keep coming at a rapid pace.

FROM HORSE TO CAR TO INTELLIGENT OBJECT

>>> The UK government has allowed driverless cars to be officially trialled on the roads since January 2015, heralding a new era of super-sophisticated transport designed to operate in a sensor-heavy, satellite-controlled, interconnected road system. By 2030, the technology is expected to reach a level of safety and sophistication that will allow all drivers to effectively become passengers as cars take over. We'll be able to work, talk to friends, or entertain ourselves on the internet as we are driven around.

Automobiles are high tech, advanced computers on wheels. They are objects way beyond the knowledge of the ordinary driver. It is increasingly impossible to service your own car not just because they contain many specialty parts, but also because the sophistication of construction of the modern automobile requires specialty tools. Even the simplest of things (changing a headlight or oil) have become complex tasks. The replacement of an oil filter on a Mercedes 190 would have cost £27.03 in 1985, whereas the 2012 Mercedes C180 leaves you with a £70 bill for oil and replacement filter, plus just over two hours of the skilled labour of a technician trained to use the specialty tools.

In 1994, replacing a headlamp on an Audi A4 cost £6.12 for the bulb and took approximately ten minutes. Today, on an equivalent model, it not only requires the purchase of a whole light cluster with a RRP (recommended retail price) of £21.56 but also 45 minutes of a trained technician's time.[50]

A car that is impossible to self-service is a Tesla. That's because it's not helpful to see it as a car. Tesla is an enhanced, sustainable energy company committed to, among other things, breakthrough travel technology. Tesla has enabled the use of an automated driving system, called Autopilot, in its Model S all-electric sedans. The wireless update of vehicles to version 7.0 of Tesla software allows properly equipped cars to steer, switch lanes, and manage speed on their own.

In a fabulously bold move, Tesla has made all its patents free to use.

The company said: "Yesterday, there was a wall of Tesla patents in the lobby of our Palo Alto headquarters. That is no longer the case. They have been removed, in the spirit of the open-source movement, for the advancement of electric vehicle technology.

Tesla Motors was created to accelerate the advent of sustainable transport. If we clear a path to the creation of compelling electric vehicles, but then lay intellectual property landmines behind us to inhibit others, we are acting in a manner contrary to that goal. "Tesla will not initiate patent lawsuits against anyone who, in good faith, wants to use our technology," the company says.[51]

We give ourselves over to the magic of technology because the benefits are so much greater. We will never expect to be able to service our own vehicles, in the same way most of us don't expect to be able to perform complex servicing tasks on our home computers. Or, for that matter, perform complex operations on our own bodies or brains!

We are not controllers of this explosive force that drives us to new places with greater knowledge and skill. We have ceded control of that to others.

COME FLY WITH ME FLY? WE CAN DO EVEN BETTER THAN THAT

Four years after the introduction of Cadillac's totally enclosed vehicle, on January 1 1914, the St. Petersburg-Tampa Airboat Line became the world's first scheduled passenger airline service. We regular Homo sapiens could walk into an airplane, sit down, "grow wings", and fly.

Flying is commonplace. We rarely see the pilots but we do hear them greeting us on board. At some point, we will let technology take the place of airplane pilots just as it has started to take the place of car drivers.

Pilotless commercial airplanes (UAVs, or Unmanned Aerial Vehicles) are already being tested and the UK company Inmarsat has started to trial high-speed global broadband, bringing the internet on board commercial flights for passenger use.[52]

Just think about this for one moment. The technology exists, and the trials are happening, whereby the people utilizing the most technology aboard planes will be the passengers. They will have access to as much airplane information as security permits. We will be flying on planes in more ways than one.

We will be technicians aboard a technical aircraft, downloading and uploading information to heighten our travel experience. It is highly unlikely that this will result in the absence of pilots. Cockpits are still places where humans make an important and valuable contribution. But it does suggest that the role of the pilot will change as technology increases.

> Now, a travel upgrade is not a better seat. It's an incredible journey through mult-dimensional time and space.

Technology flies the planes and the pilots drive the technology.

Traveling via the internet takes you farther, while at the same time allowing you to be rooted in the same place at the center of your personal web of connectivity.

We travel as constantly updated experts. The slogan of the travel company Responsible Travel is, "Travel Like a Local."[53] En route to relatively non-tourist areas, we can upload the data we need to be as knowledgeable as the locals in a heartbeat and be prepared to live and eat the way they do.

We can even communicate with them via internet-fed instant translators.[54]

There is now an explosion of travel. The SUNY LEVIN Institute has plotted that in 1980, it was estimated that 227 million people crossed international borders on airplanes. By the year 2012, international tourist arrivals reached an estimated 1,035 million people.[55] By 2020, the figure is estimated to be 1.6 billion as this chart from coolgeography.co.uk reveals (see *Figure 8*).

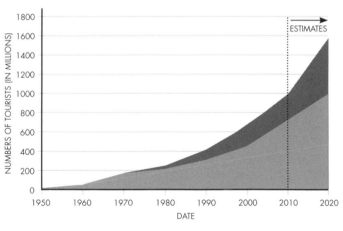

A GRAPH REVEALING APPROXIMATE TOURIST ARRIVALS IN MILLIONS

■ ASIA, AFRICA & MIDDLE EAST (MILLIONS)
■ EUROPE AND AMERICAS

FIGURE 8: MORE PEOPLE THAN EVER ARE TRAVELING BY AIR, FROM 1,035 MILLION IN 2012 TO AN ESTIMATED 1.6 BILLION IN 2020

The World Bank estimates that approximately 5 billion people are currently earning less than $10 per day.[56] This means that 70% of those who might conceivably be able to afford to fly actually do.

Of the many factors driving this increase,[57] the internet is creating the most significant effect. Access to the world via our personal cyber screens creates the desire to travel and the affordability to do so. In fact, we now merge cyberspace with real space and in so doing see a world of endless opportunities. Anywhere (safe) is fair game and our ability to construct travel plans on our own terms makes travel more than ever a uniquely personal experience. Cyberspace is a specific place for us now. The planet is specific, too, but we feel free to travel at will in cyberspace, baggage-free, visa-free, and time-free.

INTERPLANETARY INTERNET

 At a talk with internet founder Vint Cerf[58] in late 2013, Vint outlined the next major development of the internet affecting travel. This is something he has been very involved in since 2000.

Vint is moving the internet into outer space. I could barely believe my ears.[59]

"No joke," reports *Wired* magazine.[60] "The launchpads will be busy over the next decade with public and private missions aimed at Mars and other planets, the moon, asteroids, and deep space. Cerf, 56, recently joined a small team of engineers at NASA's Jet Propulsion Laboratory to begin sketching out a wireless communications network that

> We are building the internet to be size of the (known) Universe.

would let all those space-based machines and – eventually – astronauts talk to one another. For example, rovers confined to a planet's surface could use a common standard to exchange data with spacecraft from other missions whizzing by. The project, dubbed Interplanetary Internet (IPN), calls for space probes and satellites to serve as net gateways, conveying data packets to and from Earth and among themselves."

Interplanetry Internet (IPN) is something we can grasp. The idea of an interconnected outer space no longer sounds like science fiction. When the images and sounds come to us at lightning speed, they will be eagerly anticipated. That Holodeck is looking a little closer.

SPACE IS NOT THE FINAL FRONTIER – WE ARE

Cyberspace, real space, outer space, and our own personalized inner space all conform to the same rules and rituals. We accept that we donate personal data in return for freedom to travel farther. We overlook the unwanted connectivity that will come our way when we choose to go to new places. We adhere to the basic rules of "click to buy", "like", and "share" as we travel and pick up unexpected delights.

Let's be clear: this is unlike any form of travel our parents could have imagined. Born in the early 1920s, my father called traveling to France "going to the Continent," revealing that particular generation's understanding of geographical confines, definitions, and terminology.

When we switch on our computers we are "going online".

When we are looking for things, we are "searching", "trawling", and "surfing", words that bear witness to our understanding that we are embarking on a journey of enormous scope, immeasurable depth, and boundless distance.

Yet we do it with ease. We feel it is largely un-policed (except for the obvious requirements of child saftey, the law, and common decency) and we feel that we have a high level of freedom to go where we like.

It's a space so essential that governments protect it from invasion because the inability to travel on the internet would render us powerless, nationally and personally.

The physicality of travel is now matched by the mental ability to take ourselves – and be taken – into new thinking and ideas through new forms of connectivity.

The experts predict big leaps in real and virtual travel through heightened interconnectivity, both explicitly seen and implicitly accepted.

David Clark, a senior research scientist at MIT's Computer Science and Artificial Intelligence Laboratory, has noted that, "Devices will more and more have their own patterns of communication, their own 'social networks,' which they use to share and aggregate information, and undertake automatic control and activation. More and more, humans will be in a world in which decisions are being made by an active set of cooperating devices. The internet (and computer-mediated communication in general) will become more pervasive but less explicit and visible. It will, to some extent, blend into the background of all we do."[61]

Joe Touch, director at the University of Southern California's Information Sciences Institute, predicted, "The internet will shift from the place we find cat videos to a background capability that will be a seamless part of how we live our everyday lives. We won't think about 'going online' or 'looking on the internet' for something – we'll just be online and just look."[62]

Bryan Alexander, senior fellow at the National Institute for Technology in Liberal Education, writes, "It will be a world more integrated than ever before. We will see more planetary friendships, rivalries, romances, work teams, study groups, and collaborations."[63] Bryan's vision will be close when Facebook links every human on the planet.

Paul Jones, a professor at the University of North Carolina and founder of ibiblio.org, believes that, "Television lets us see the global village, but the internet lets us be actual villagers."[64]

Augmented and virtual reality experts "Inition" have been demonstrating the potential for technology like Oculus Rift to transport us, or even "teleport" us, to amazing destinations. In their laboratory in Shoreditch, East London, they have constructed "virtual catwalks" for fashion retailer

Top Shop, created immersive stereoscopic 360° land-scapes for us to inhabit, and have thrown people out of planes at 15,000 feet–virtually, of course–but the experience is very real.[65]

Marriott Hotels is giving a similar glimpse into the future of travel, but to those who really don't like to travel. The hotel chain is also using the Oculus Rift headset and a phone booth-like structure equipped with the odours and sensations of an exotic locale to create a "4D" experience. In practice, that means strapping on an Oculus Rift that feeds you visions of Hawaiian beaches or downtown London, while the booth conjures up mist, odours, and heat related to what you're seeing. For instance, if you're seeing visions of a shoreline in Hawaii, you might feel a cool, moist breeze.

BEAM ME UP, SCOTTY

 Marriot dubbed this "The Teleporter," wisely nodding to the magical world of *Star Trek* and science fiction.

The Teleporter is part of Marriott's "Travel Brilliantly" campaign, which launched in 2013 and seeks to engage consumers in a dialogue about how the chain can make travel "more brilliant." To answer that question, Marriott has collaborated with the MIT Mobile Experience Lab, among other partners.[66] It is just the sort of collision of business, science, and technology that we can expect to see more of in the years ahead.

Magical it may seem, but a version of teleportation is very real. Scientists from the Hasso Plattner Institute in Potsdam have invented a real-life teleporter system that can scan in an object and "beam it" to another location.[67] Scotty (another a nod to *Star Trek*) is a simple self-contained appliance that allows teleporting inanimate physical objects across distances.

Not quite the dematerialisation and reconstruction models of science fiction, the system relies on destructive scanning and 3D printing.

An object at one end of the system is milled down layer by layer, creating a scan per layer, which is then transmitted through an encrypted communication to a 3D printer. The printer then replicates the original object layer by layer, effectively teleporting an object from one place to another.

Facebook's purchase of Oculus Rift for $2 billion was a strategic reach into the post-mobile world.

"Immersive virtual and augmented reality will become a part of people's everyday lives," Facebook's founder, Mark Zuckerberg, said. "History suggests there will be more platforms to come, and whoever builds and defines these will shape the future and reap the benefits."[68]

A post-mobile world of immersive interconnectivity is now with us. We will "travel like a local" indeed. And eat, live, and talk like locals. Instantly.

TIME IS MOVING FASTER. NO. IT *REALLY* IS.

 Our notion of time presents difficulties. Time is not a sense like smell, sight, and touch. We don't so much "sense" time as perceive it.

And our perception of time is changing. The simple equation for speed provides the clue (see *Figure 9*).

$$\text{SPEED} = \frac{\text{DISTANCE}}{\text{TIME}}$$

FIGURE 9: ALTHOUGH THE INTERNET HAS GIVEN US THE ABILITY TO TRAVEL FARTHER THAN EVER BEFORE FROM OUR OWN COMPUTERS, THE TIME IN WHICH WE CAN TRAVEL REMAINS A CONSTANT

The ancient Greeks and Romans used the changing seasons to remind them of the advance of time.[69] Medieval sundials remind us of the effect of the daily arc of the sun on our lives. Each change in the arc claims one of the hours. The phrase *omnes vulnerant, ultima necat* (they all wound us, but the last kills) is often found inscribed on sundials.

It is also principally from sundials that we get the aphorism *tempus fugit*, or time flies! And time certainly flies when you're having fun on the internet.

The internet has gifted us with the ability to increase the distance we travel in terms of places we visit and things we discover. But, of course, the time in which we can do the long-distance travel remains a constant.

Therefore, we perceive that we are moving faster.

> Inner space, outer space, virtual space, real space. There are no barriers.

The internet is speeding up travel faster than any new motorized technology. The distances we go will be greater, including into outer space. And the manner of our travel will be as natural as visiting a friend who lives around the corner.

It is as if we were one giant supernova bursting into many different directions at breakneck speed. And because of the speed, we are constantly checking our navigation or status—in fact, we consult our phones up to 150 times a day.[70] We spend almost six hours a day on the internet, searching and transacting as much as we can, as fast as we can.[71]

It's a frenetic pace and to make sense of where we can go, we need a map. The maps we have right now send us to places (Google), pay for services (banks, Apple Pay), describe places (Wikipedia) or give peer reviews (Trip Advisor). These technologies are "part one" internet technologies. They are intermediary technology stepping in to assist, oversee, and govern our cyberspace journeys. They are wonderful, helpful inventions, but with the speed at which we are traveling to myriad destinations, we need more.

We need a trusted map and not one that only we can believe in, but one that is trusted by everybody. We have all experienced the nervousness of buying something from a new online retailer, or maybe booking a room in an unknown place, or even riding in a small airplane in a foreign country. Will they stick with their refund agreement? Will they have the room I booked when I turn up or will it be double booked?

The first of potentially many new maps arrived quietly at the end of 2008.

ANOTHER USE
OF BLOCKCHAIN[72]

 Blockchain, as we saw in chapter one, is a new form of Internet Protocol, as new as the arrival of HTML in late 1991 that kick-started the internet as we know it today.

While its first major application has been to drive and record transactions for the crypto-currency Bitcoin, it has uses way beyond crypto-currencies.

Simply put, Blockchain works like this. All subscribers have the software on their personal computers. Everyone has exactly the same software and can see it being updated by transactions. So when one transaction happens, the software is universally updated. Exactly the same transaction cannot happen twice because the entire ecosystem would reject a clone. There would be no room for it on the "universal ledger".

For example, if it were to record an attachment sent by email, it would note that an email has been sent with an attachment. Everybody in the network would know that the attachment has gone from A to B. If the same attachment was sent again by the original sender (A), the transaction would fail. Why? Because the original sender does not have it anymore. The attachment is now with the original recipient (B).

It is the simplicity, universality, and transparency that makes blockchain so compelling.

Before blockchain, we had to rely on trusted third parties to verify our transactions. You might call your bank to ask if the money reached the recipient, who was denying its arrival.

Blockchain is not yet used much beyond bitcoin transactions. But it will be. And it will enable unknown places to be more accessible, journeys to be more effortless, and global transactions to be a whole lot safer.

TRAVEL SAFE

 So much of "where we go" online is safe. We don't need online embassies to offer advice or warnings. In fact, we don't need passports, visas, or immunizations. The internet is a borderless community and we can easily choose to have our own built-in virus scanners.

However, threat still exists.

In the UK, online banking fraud increased by 71% in 2014, compared to the previous year. Spamming, phishing, and spear phishing are all huge, widespread, online dangers.

Spamming is unsolicited e-mail, often of a commercial nature, sent indiscriminately to multiple mailing lists, individuals, or newsgroups. It's also known as junk e-mail.

Phishing is the act of sending an email to a user falsely claiming to be an established, legitimate enterprise in an attempt to scam the user into surrendering private information that will be used for identity theft.

Spear-phishing is one of the main tools used by attackers to compromise technology endpoints in large company computer systems and gain a foothold in the enterprise's network (the main computer software drivers that run the daily actions of a company). The attacker utilizes a specially crafted e-mail message that lures users to perform an action that will result in malware infection and possible theft of critical and private data.

Such an attack happened to the UK company, Talk Talk, in October 2015.

Symantec, the global software security company, estimates the daily e-mail spam volume to be in the region of 29 billion.[73] Yes, daily. Symantec also calculates the number of web attacks blocked every day to be 568,700.

In fact, cyber security experts Mandiant Fire/Eye believe that more than 95% of networks are compromised in some way.[74]

But we are blissfully unaware of any of this most of the time. In fact, 69% of online fraud victims learn from a third party – such as their bank or online retailer – that they have been compromised,.

While not at all diminishing the danger and distress that cyber attacks can cause, this does not resemble being held up by a highwayman or robbed in a resort hotel.

In fact, while the attackers are smart, well equipped and determined, there is no reason that the defence systems can't be equally smart.

The hackers have replaced the highwaymen, but our travel today is no more financially risky and certainly a great deal more comfortable.

We have elevated the idea of travel to new heights, breadths, and depths. Anthropology records the magnificent migratory journeys of our early ancestors. History records the expansion of ancient empires and the adventures of Marco Polo, Vasco da Gama, Christopher Columbus, and Neil Armstrong. Now the internet records our incredible journeys day-by-day, hour-by-hour, minute-by-minute, and second-by-second.

Our trips into other people's lives, across the ocean or out into the universe are tracked, traced, and stored. We leave our virtual footprints everywhere, revealing where we are crossing paths with others, ending up in the same place as our friends or going down blind alleys.

Laws like the UK's Investigatory Powers Bill make our journeys through cyberspace open for review.

The law requires phone and web companies to store records of websites visited by every citizen for 12 months. These visits can then be accessed and reviewed by police, security services, and other public bodies.

This provides nation states with an obvious level of security satisfaction. Those against such intrusion regard such legislation as "snooper's charter"; those less concerned see it as a safety precaution.

> Curiously, travel is less about moving. It is captured and stored. It is securely held. Travel stays still.

My British Airways online club membership can tell me every country I visited since I joined the club, how many miles I flew, and on what precise date my journey took place. When I think about where I have been, or when asked about details of my trips, I can recall them with extraordinary exactitude. The data doesn't change with age, isn't lost to memory, or mutated in any way over time. I can call upon locals to add flavour to advice you might need. I can return to those places in an instant.

The point about this data is not so much that it exists, but that it redefines our travel away from flux, transitoriness, and ephemerality. Now travel is permanent. It is captured, stored, filmed, and filed. It is securely held.

Curiously, travel, in addition to being fast, effortless, and omnipresent, is also immobile. When we have travelled and returned, we can still be there.

I don't mean to engage you in some arcane philosophical conundrum; I just mean to express this thought. We have so extended ourselves that we can site ourselves in places we have already left and in which we no longer physically exist. And while we are sited in those places, we can continue to converse and explore through the power of automation.

We are travelling more than ever while staying in the same place.

Try explaining that to our earlier human prototype – our most recent ancestors.

WE THE (PROFESSIONAL) PEOPLE

MAKE IT CONVENIENT, STUPID

Everyone has heard of Amazon.com. But not everyone has heard of Piggly Wiggly (or Morrisons, or Carrefour, or Edeka–you get the point).

Piggly Wiggly was the first true self-service grocery store. Clarence Saunders founded it on September 6 1916, at 79 Jefferson Avenue in Memphis, Tennessee. Self-service eventually spread across the globe and changed everything, including the way food was presented, offered, and stored.

In the UK, sales of deep frozen food quadrupled between 1955 and 1960 as self service stores gained ground. The following year, UK research company Market Investigations Ltd interviewed 2,000 housewives (by standing outside their front doors) about many aspects of their grocery shopping habits.[75] In 1961, 40% now shopped just once a week (compared with 35% in 1957) and also for

40% of the sample, Friday was the main shopping day. In 1957, 52% had always gone to the same store; by 1961 it was only 27%. And it was younger shoppers setting the trend.

Convenience was to become a byword for all types of shopping. And convenience is the calling card of online businesses such as Amazon.

Amazon is the largest online retailer in the world, with 244 million active customers in 2014 (an impressive 14% increase from the previous year),[76] producing $74.4 billion in revenue. The Chinese e-commerce company Alibaba.com has more customers (302 million), but, with a different business model, has much less revenue ($8.4 billion).

It's not unusual for large stores to have many millions of customers (Wal-Mart serves 245 million customers weekly worldwide). But here's the obvious difference: Amazon has just one store. Wal-Mart has over 11,000.

But the impact of Amazon and Alibaba is not the growth figures, or number of customers, or indeed the market penetration. It is the way they have dominated a fundamental shift in the way we shop.

It's not a shift characterized by e-commerce, per se. It is a shift characterized by an intrinsic remodelling of our shopping habits.

In fact, the percentage of online shopping in most established markets barely gets into double digits.

You would think, given the prevalence of discussion that abounds, that we all shopped, all the time, online. But we don't. We do something far more "shape-shifting" in terms of habit-forming routine.

An April 2013 survey by Dimensional Research[77] of 1,046 active shoppers revealed that an overwhelming 90% of respondents who recalled reading online reviews claimed that positive online reviews influenced buying decisions, while 86% said that buying decisions were influenced by negative online reviews.

The survey demonstrated convincingly that customer service – both good and bad – impacts revenue, with participants ranking customer service as the number-one factor impacting vendor trust.

After a positive customer service experience, 62% of business-to-business (B2B) and 42% of business-to-consumer (B2C) customers purchased more.

After a negative customer service interaction, 66% of B2B and 52% of B2C customers stopped buying. And 95% shared their bad experiences with others, while 87% shared their good experiences with others (see *Figure 10*).

HOW THE CUSTOMER HAS PROGRESSED

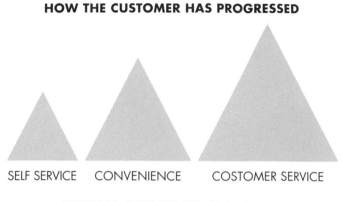

SELF SERVICE   CONVENIENCE   COSTOMER SERVICE

FIGURE 10: CUSTOMER SERVICE IS NOW THE NUMBER-ONE FACTOR AFFECTING VENDOR TRUST.

The effect of the internet on our choices of products, method of purchase, and brand loyalty has been the explosion of two new behaviours: both facets of shopping that were once a small, personal and often ill-informed part of our psyche.

Customers have become procurers.

And consumers have become prosumers.

Let's take these in turn.

PROCURERS

 We procure our products using fast and easy-to-use online tools that can be with us at all times. These tools are agile, and they can respond to serendipitous chance or last-minute requests. They also acknowledge our important strategic and regular requirements.

These tools allow us to audit for peer verification, analyze for competitive weaknesses, qualify with experts, collate for price comparison, budget for financial prudence, and search multiple supply chains for speed, efficiency, quality, and price.

It is a step change – a giant leap forward – and for the first time reconfigures every aspect of our "old" notion of shopping. How much things cost, why, and whether they could be cheaper are questions we can ask and, more importantly, answer.

The quality of items – holiday experiences, for example – can be audited and cross-referenced.

Procurement is shopping that is energized and enhanced by the internet. Procurement is about winning and securing beneficial relationships. It's about getting exactly what we want, because we have the tools to do what we want (see *Figure 11*).

It is the "consumerization" of IT (information technology).

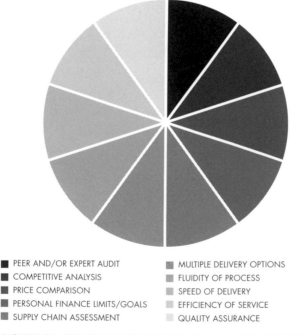

PEER AND/OR EXPERT AUDIT
COMPETITIVE ANALYSIS
PRICE COMPARISON
PERSONAL FINANCE LIMITS/GOALS
SUPPLY CHAIN ASSESSMENT

MULTIPLE DELIVERY OPTIONS
FLUIDITY OF PROCESS
SPEED OF DELIVERY
EFFICIENCY OF SERVICE
QUALITY ASSURANCE

FIGURE 11: CONSUMERS HAVE BECOME PROCURERS OF PRODUCTS AND SERVICES, USING ALL THE ONLINE TOOLS AT THEIR DISPOSAL.

Procurers today have never been more aware of pricing and what they're willing to spend. In fact, more than 50% of consumers say they know the prices that they pay and notice when prices change. Consumers will continue this expectation of value for their money when shopping at modern convenience stores, as this chart from The Nielsen Company reveals (see *Figure 12*).

PRICE SENSITIVITY IN EUROPE
EUROPEAN SHOPPERS

6%	Have no idea of prices or price changes
38%	Not aware of prices, but notice all changes
40%	Know most prices and notice all changes
16%	Know prices of all items regularly purchased

SOURCE: NIELSEN SHOPPER TRENDS EUROPE 2014

FIGURE 12: THE MAJORITY OF PROCURERS KNOW HOW MUCH THEY PAY FOR GOODS AND SERVICES, AND WHEN THOSE PRICES CHANGE.

By definition, our relationship with retailers and service suppliers has changed. They have suffered a jolt and the more enlightened ones are responding by attempting to understand each and every one of us in a detailed, granular way.

The first thing organizations do is study and understand the rapid growth in consumer expertise and expectations, reorganize to manage it – and hopefully stay ahead of it. It is complex and different, because dealing with procurers is not at all like dealing with compliant customers.

Ultimately this consumer shift requires one over-arching company change: all businesses must now behave like tech brands.

THE GEEKS ARE IN THE BOARDROOM

 Some organizations today are creating new posts like chief digital officer. Look at the staggering leap in numbers in the chart opposite (see *Figure 13*).

Equally staggering is the number of company CEOs that have come from a direct "tech" background, as *Inc.* magazine has pointed out.[78]

Instagram's CEO, Kevin Systrom, was a self-taught programmer. Facebook's CEO, Mark Zuckerberg, began writing software before entering high school, and still keeps a hand in coding today.

Dropbox CEO, Drew Houston, wrote the first lines of code for his company while in a Boston train station. WordPress cofounder (and founder and CEO of WordPress's parent company, Automattic), Matt Mullenweg,

NUMBER OF CHIEF DIGITAL OFFICERS WORLDWIDE

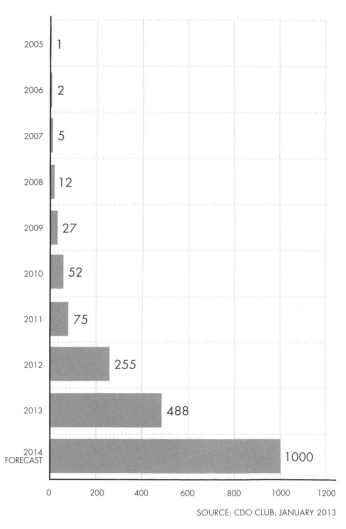

SOURCE: CDO CLUB, JANUARY 2013

FIGURE 13: NEW JOB POSITIONS, SUCH AS CHIEF DIGITAL
OFFICER, ARE INCREASING BY HUGE NUMBERS.

used his technical skills to help build the democratic publishing platform from the ground up.

Microsoft's Bill Gates, Amazon's Jeff Bezos, Google's Larry Page ... the list goes on. Each of these leaders possessed a deep understanding of the technology that their business was built upon.

According to a PwC Survey of US CEOs: "When business leaders considered the megatrends rocking our world, 86% cited technological advances as the global trend that will most transform business."[79]

The techies who were once in the basements of organizations are now moving up to the executive suite and providing solutions about how the procurers are now shopping, by gathering our data and creating internet-enabled tools to assist us.

TATA Consultancy Services provide extensive data on the digital initiatives at more than 800 major companies around the world, and they have provided numerous insights on their strategies, impacts, investments, and future plans.[80]

"Companies in 13 global industries across four regions of the world see their digital initiatives as crucial to business success this decade, and, as a result, they are making major investments. Some 70% say their digital initiatives are either the most important factor in their firm's success or of 'major' importance."

"Overall, [these] companies will invest an average of $113 million this year in digital initiatives that give them an online connection to customers and the products they sell to them. All [of these] companies, on average, plan to maintain their spending through 2017 (with projected average spending of $111 million)."

"A select group of companies (4%) will spend at least $1 billion each this year on digital initiatives, and the same percentage plan to spend as much in 2017."

"A vast majority of companies (95%) see digital technologies as a critical way to connect to their customers and are already doing so through mobile apps, monitoring social media comments, providing downloadable digital products, and other means."

> To succeed in the future, all companies must become tech companies.

This is the case for both B2C and B2B companies.

"The three industries making the biggest digital investments in 2014 (media, telecom, and conventional technology companies) are more likely to reinvent their business models and bring digital products to market than the other sectors. But more than a third of companies in retail, insurance, banking, and utilities believe they too will need to 'digitally reimagine' their businesses by the end of the decade."

> # Companies are turning to smart tech as shoppers turn to smart devices.

"Big Data is central to digital initiatives. Over the next three years, companies worldwide will spend more of their digital budgets on Big Data and analytics technology to understand their customers' digital habits. The greatest percentage of spending on the digital five forces will go to Big Data and analytics, which will command 28% of the digital technology budget, followed by mobile devices (20%), social media (20%), cloud computing (19%), and artificial intelligence and robotics (13%). The fact that Big Data and analytics investments are larger than those for the other digital forces shows just how critical Big Data has become to corporate success."

By 2020, a majority of companies predict they will gather customer data through multiple channels.

Tata Consultancy Services have also provided us with some key examples of how companies across the world are gathering (or plan to gather) digital data from customers[81] (see *Figure 14*).

HOW COMPANIES GATHER DATA
FROM THEIR CUSTOMERS

Via wearable digital devices or devices that end customers can attach to other products not made by the respondent's company

Via digital sensors and/or other digital devices embedded in or attached to company's products used by customers

Via digital products that the company sells and distributes online to customers' computers

Via other digital online connections to customers

Via continuous monitoring and analysis of customers' comments in public social media sites

Via mobile apps for customers' devices

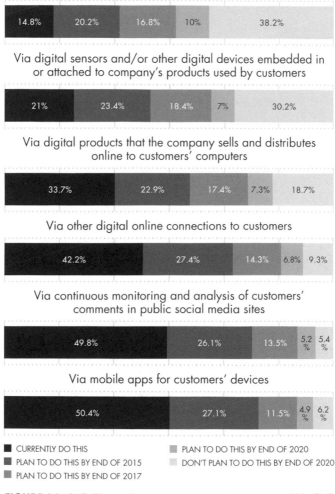

FIGURE 14: GATHERING CUSTOMER DATA IS A MAJOR INVESTMENT PRIORITY FOR MANY COMPANIES OVER THE NEXT FEW YEARS.

But businesses beware!

Just bringing in expertise is not enough. To succeed, businesses must change the way they work and think.

All "pre-Google" companies will have IT infrastructures designed to manage customers (and employees) from a different era. Payroll management, stock inventory systems, CRM (Customer Relationship Management) programs, and internal communications are all obvious candidates for the kind of role IT conventionally plays.

But stack these up against the requirements of the modern procurer and they decidedly fall short. Companies need to instrument and optimize their systems for the Internet of Things and for the proliferation of hardware that will further feed its growth.

It's easy if you are Airbnb or Uber, for example. These two together now stand as the poster children for liberated, agile, billion-dollar, mass-market businesses.

It is frightening (for long established companies) to think of the speed of their growth versus their pre-Google forefathers. It is even more frightening to imagine the next generation of disintermediating concepts just around the corner.[82]

The diagram opposite (often referred to as "Bi-Model IT") explains now companies must now adapt to keep abreast (see *Figure 15*).

TAKING THE COMPETITIVE LEAP

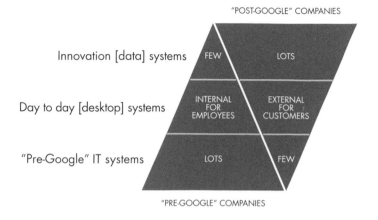

FIGURE 15: PRE-GOOGLE COMPANIES ARE NOW ADAPTING
THEIR IT DEPARTMENTS TO STAY COMPETITIVE.

An intriguing game is being played. Shoppers are procuring through access to more data and an enhanced "always-on" experience, and service suppliers and retailers are examining each and every personal commercial motive with a view to bringing bespoke tech solutions to the process.

At the first suggestion that we cannot find what we want, we jump ship to another vendor. But in a nanosecond we can be offered two or three alternatives or persuaded into a different product or service before we move on.

This new game needs new skills and new rules.

So we are learning how to optimize decision-making to ensure we have purchased the right product. We are learning how to optimize data usage and manage the data outflow from our devices with the data inflow from persistent retailers and service providers.

And we will have to learn how and where we can acquire and use new tools that short-circuit some of the difficulties inherent in the first two skills above.

Decision-making is actually a complex science and was first mathematically expressed by the Reverend Thomas Bayes in the early 18th century. The "Bayes Theorem"[83] and online decision-making is well covered by Askew and Coovert, who make the point that online decision-making is a complex process that will take time to understand.[84] But they make the point that it is not following a classic paradigm (e.g., Bayes). Rather, the focus tends to be on how the medium might be impacting a decision outcome.

The new breed of "business consumers" needs to (and wants to) evaluate their own commercial success when basing purchasing decision-making on their various devices. How does mobile technology compare to computer-, or retail-driven technology such as iBeacon? Our devices simplify payments and enable on-site offers, but they also build our own purchasing desires into an automated process.

iBeacon already offers a number of technology opportunities to customers merging, again, personal private benefits with workplace benefits. Here's how iBeacon sells its service:[85]

- At a music festival, your phone creates a playlist based on which bands you saw.

- At a restaurant, your phone recommends certain foods based on how many calories you've burned that day. Ran three miles this morning? Go ahead, have dessert.

- At the mall, your phone alerts you that a new style you previously liked is finally in stock.

- A doctor knows his patient's exact status, just by walking into a hospital room.

- At a conference for work? Your phone knows which panels and keynotes you attended and aggregates presentation materials for you.

- At a ball game, your phone tells you how likely you are to catch a foul ball or home run based on where you're sitting.

- At the train station, your phone senses you're on the platform and tells you if your train is on time or delayed, and where to stand to get the car with the most available seats.

- At the airport, your phone beams you a map of nearby power outlets, tells you if your flight is delayed, and of any deals that might be offered by stores in the terminal.

> We are upgraded shoppers. But we need to learn how to use our new skills.

The entire process is built on a mutual exchange of data.

By 2020, the US government may have put guidelines in place specifying how data-collectors – from app developers to advertising networks to operating system makers like Google, Apple, and BlackBerry – must disclose the data they collect and how it will be used. The push for a so-called "Apps Act" in the US grew out of a report issued by the Federal Trade Commission in early 2013. Among its findings:

"Less than one-third of Americans feel they are in control of their personal information on their mobile devices."

Exactly how much of our "personal data" we are prepared to give up is a matter of huge conjecture. Almost certainly the issue is not about, "How much data do they have?" but "What are they doing with it?"

We will have to learn about acquiring tools and developing skill sets to optimize our product purchasing patterns. Target, the US retailer, offers an interesting tool to its customers. "Cartwheel" is Target's smartphone app that lets you scan items as you put them in your basket to comparison shop for savings.

Wal-Mart has "Savings Catcher", which lets you compare your end receipt against a database of competitors' specials. The difference – the amount you overpaid – is refunded on a gift card redeemable on your next trip to Wal-Mart. And that's part of the point: to get you to come back to the store. Apple's Apple Pay was first tested inside the Apple stores for an independent, stress- and friction-free experience.

And Amazon.com has Amazon Prime, a multi-layered program that combines volume discounts with free shipping, media downloads, music streaming and video streaming a la Netflix.

But procurers are more than enhanced online shoppers. "Where" they receive their information is as important as "how" they receive it.

Fixed-line telephony and television, a staple in households from the mid 1950s, rooted remote conversation and broadcast transmissions in the home. Reception rooms, designed to formally receive people, morphed into living rooms as the TV flickered like a warming fire in the corner of everyone's communal room.

Advertising was pumped directly into the home by TV, radio, and the newspaper delivery boy.[86] Salespeople had to wait on the doorstep, outside the home.

Outside the home, poster advertising was seen as a reinforcement of the mainstream messages communicated by

TV and newspaper advertising. For other sales messages, you had to enter the marketplace itself for competitive offers ("bananas half price," "six oranges for the price of two"). Market traders most often shouted these offers, while in-store deals were found on hastily written cardboard hanging from the ceiling as near to the promotional item as possible.

Marketing was essentially an in-home experience and it was in the home that products were discussed and debated. Sometimes the debate would be taken into the back garden, where it was strengthened by over-the-fence conversation or washing-day gossip.

Today marketing has moved out of home. It is carried out on our many devices and travels with us wherever we go. Newspaper delivery has declined[87] and time-shift TV is rising inexorably as we choose to watch a piece of content as opposed to watching fixed TV.[88]

"Out of home" means being wherever you are. So to follow you, there is a rise in the use of social media advertising. In truth, today only a fraction of retailers' online sales are actually generated directly through a referral from a social network. But the volume of social commerce is growing quickly, in the triple digits in many cases. Overall, social commerce sales grew at three times the rate of overall e-commerce from 2013 to 2014.[89]

Out of home is the new battlefield for our hearts and minds, and this is having an unexpected effect.

Bricks and mortar retailers, whose prophesied demise (and actual, in some cases, as seen with Borders, Blockbuster, HMV, and Woolworths) was once a boon to gumptious, go-getting online retailers, are now free to compete on their own territory–out of home–but with the advantage of internet-enabled technology. Not all are competing, but those that are employ a range of tactics. And they can be both giant retailers and small local stores.

In June 2014, the UK government announced it was kick-starting an initiative to create apps designed to help struggling local retailers compete.[90] Projects included an attempt to build a virtual version of Leeds's Kirkgate Market, where shoppers could buy online and pick up their purchases later at the ornate building where Marks & Spencer was founded.[91] Another service allowed shoppers to view special offers in shop windows via a virtual reality tool.

But the future looks even more interesting.

Procurers today, with a sharp learning curve, have become natural voyagers in cyberspace.

"Cyberspace" is a relatively modern term[92] and has been accelerated as a notion by the arrival of the internet, as this albeit crude Google Ngram reveals (see *Figure 16* over the page).

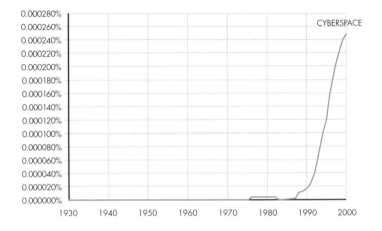

FIGURE 16: THE WORD 'CYBERSPACE' IS NO LONGER
SCIENCE FICTION AND IS COMMONLY USED.

The idea of "how we live" in cyberspace is becoming an important area of academic research, drawing in eminent experts not least from the fields of psychoanalysis and psychotherapy.[93] It is not the remit of this book to add to that particular debate.

But one area is of significance with regard to procurers. Professor Alessandra Lemma, in a September 2014 paper,[94] writes: "If we adopt then, for example, Delueze's suggestion[95] that 'the virtual is opposed not to the real but to the actual' (1994: 208) then the virtual is fully real insofar as it is virtual. Moreover, this kind of virtuality may represent a necessary step toward the realm of what is possible. In other words, it may contain the seeds for imagining oneself as different and hence for being different. Here the real may be seen as partial, flawed while the virtual promises a resolution to come, which may then be experimented with in virtual reality before being actualized in reality."

As procurers in cyberspace, mobilized to act by the accommodation of internet-enabled tools, driven to precision by data flows in and out of our devices, and inspired by a new level of convenience and self-service, we will see our new behaviours as operating in a new retail reality.

Augmented-reality retail fixtures, virtual reality demonstrations, and interconnected digital sensors and devices will merge with our "always-on" internet interconnectedness. And as procurers, we will live as much in the virtual world as the actual world, both of them being very real to us.

PROSUMERS

 In their 1972 book, *Take Today*, Marshall McLuhan and Barrington Nevitt foresaw that with "electric technology" humans would be able to produce their own goods as well as buy goods from stores and, indeed, other individual producers. It was a prescient prediction of the age of the prosumer.

But the actual term "prosumer" was first coined by the futurologist Alvin Toffler in his 1980 book, *The Third Wave*. Toffler's "proactive consumers" – prosumers – were regular consumers who were predicted to help personally improve or design the goods and services of the marketplace, transforming it and their roles as consumers (see *Figure 17*).[96]

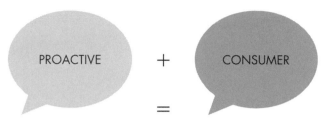

PROSUMER

FIGURE 17: PROSUMERS ARE ACTIVE CONSUMERS WHO PERSONNALY INTERVENE IN COMPANIES AND THEREFORE TRANSFORM PRODUCTS, SERVICES AND THE ROLE OF THE CONSUMER

We consumers are becoming prosumers because we are freely giving up valuable information to companies and are becoming more sophisticated in our demands. This information helps companies adapt products and services and allows them to integrate these into as many different consumer profiles as is possible.

The impact on businesses is fundamental. Once, consumers were people "on the outside" that you had to sell to. They needed to be observed. Sometimes you would ask them questions about what you were doing to see if they agreed. In every business I worked, consumers were talked about as if they were a different species, ignoring the famous adman David Ogilvy's (albeit dated) advice: "The consumer is not a moron, she's your wife."

The integrated way in which people interact with companies means that today's consumer is as much a part of the organization as the employees within it. In fact, it is not a difficult leap to say that the shift to the prosumer has re-assigned conventional internal departments almost to the status of supplier.

Smart organizations will respond and adapt their products and services instantly to the behaviour and demands of the integrated prosumer. What facilitates this is the profusion of consumer-centric technologies, interlinked and driven by the internet. Cisco provides a picture of this growth in device-to-device interconnectivity (see *Figure 18*):

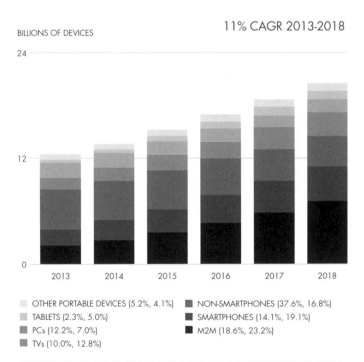

FIGURE 18: BILLIONS OF DEVICES INTERCONNECT WITH EACH OTHER.

Often called the "Internet Of Things" (IOT), this machine-to-machine connectivity is not only allowing stores to talk to warehouses and warehouses to talk to smartphones, it allows products to talk to each other. In fact, any object can be embedded with software that enables those objects to collect and exchange data (see *Figure 19*).

ONCE YOU START, EVERYTHING STARTS TALKING TO EVERYTHING ELSE

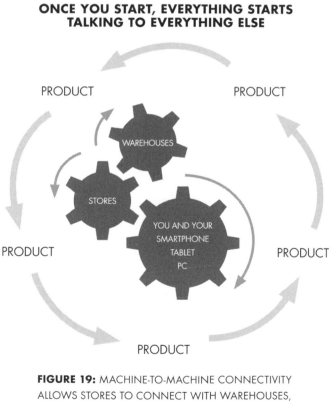

FIGURE 19: MACHINE-TO-MACHINE CONNECTIVITY ALLOWS STORES TO CONNECT WITH WAREHOUSES, AND WAREHOUSES TO SMARTPHONES.

So engulfing will be the IOT that consulting firm McKinsey is projecting a staggering potential economic impact of between $3.9 trillion and $11.1 trillion annually by 2025.[97]

When I order something from Amazon on my smartphone, there is no smiling salesperson to take my order. I am simply plucking what I want directly from the warehouse and giving instructions as to where I would like it delivered. Instantly Amazon adapts its messaging to me, blending in my most recent purchase to my history. If you want a quick image of your purchasing patterns and lifestyle DNA, take a look at your Amazon personalized home page and it will tell you immediately. It is also a clear picture of your "presumptions" demonstrating how Amazon has reshaped itself around your needs.

Airline apps that let you create your own boarding pass and allow you to choose your seat are doing the same thing. You are issuing the boarding pass to yourself. Therefore you are instantly working for the airline and being a customer at the same time.

Alongside the growth of IOT, we will see an explosion of internet-enabled devices. In fact, expect hardware growth to match that of the software growth of the last few years and follow Moore's exponential growth laws.

To turn a consumer into a prosumer brings enormous advantages to companies. They really do create an intimate commercial relationship, and if they hone the interaction perfectly, prosumers will be delighted by the apparent bespoke service they are receiving. Such mutuality brings with it enormous financial benefit. Companies can now live in the pockets of their customers and be ready to serve up personalized sales at the touch of a screen. The development of cheaper and more versatile 3D printing technologies will further spur this growth.

Later in the book, we shall show how the power of internet-enabled technology can touch people in a magical way.

We have entered an age where we are acquiring and procuring, bringing together multiple data streams, uniting virtual and actual worlds, and making winning purchase decisions with the dexterity of expert retailers.

> Companies must recognise that they are service departments for professional consumers.

In creating procurers and prosumers, the internet has upturned a centuries-old transactional sales process and created an upgraded professional shopper.

Few retailers are talking to shoppers in this way, but then few retailers who were focused on self-service a hundred years ago thought about convenience. Procurers and prosumers are more than a progression of shopping habits; they are a material change in the psyche of modern buyers and in the development of consumer-friendly IT (see *Figure 20*).

They are superbly enabled shoppers, a new breed, if you like, and as each new internet-enabled technology arrives, they grow more able and more confident.

THE CONSUMERISATION OF IT HAS REDEFINED EXPECTATIONS

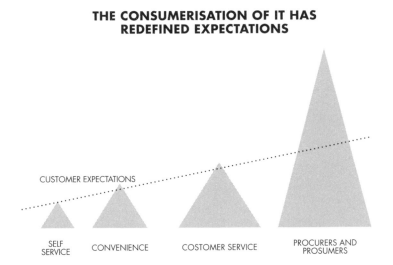

FIGURE 20: THE INTERNET HAS TURNED CONSUMERS INTO PROFESSIONAL SHOPPERS, WITH INCREASED EXPECTATIONS FOR CUSTOMER SERVICE AND THE SHOPPING EXPERIENCE.

INDUSTRIOUS
LEISURE

Not everyone has access to the internet.[98] But soon everyone will.

On June 1 2014 a source close to Google announced that Google would spend $1 billion on 180 satellites to bring global internet access to the remaining two-thirds of the planet that does not have access (approximately 4.8 billion people).[99]

This followed a similar statement of intent the previous year, in August 2013, by Mark Zuckerberg of Facebook. Zuckerberg wants everyone on Earth connected to the internet, because he believes that access to the internet is a human right.

He's not alone. Access to the internet should be a basic Human Right, thinks the United Nations, which on May 16 2011 issued communiqué A/HRC/17/27, stating:

"Given that the internet has become an indispensable tool for realizing a range of human rights, combating inequality, and accelerating development and human progress, ensuring universal access to the internet should be a priority for all states." It goes on to say that, as a basic human right, disconnecting people from the internet would be a human rights violation and against international law.

Few, except despots, tyrants, and dictators, would argue that access to the internet should be denied. But most agree that access to certain content should be restricted or disallowed. Here, certain pornography, child protection, and seditious or stolen material are obvious contenders.

Once we have access to the internet, it quickly becomes an intrinsic part of our physical makeup. It becomes a physiological need every bit as important as sleep, shelter, sex, and warmth.[100] As such, it plays a natural and dominant role in our leisure time.

Its biggest impact is on what enough.org (a website developed in 1994 to make the internet safer) has revealed is our insatiable desire for pornography. Porn sites get more visitors each month than Netflix, Amazon, and Twitter combined.

In fact, a monumental 30% of the internet industry is pornography and mobile porn is expected to reach $2.8 billion by 2015.[101]

The United States is the largest producer and exporter of hard-core pornographic DVDs and web material, followed by Germany.[102]

A Google trends analysis indicates that searches for "teen porn" have more than tripled between 2005 and 2013. Total searches for teen-related porn reached an estimated 500,000 daily in March 2013 – one-third of total daily searches for pornographic websites.

Of the 304 scenes analyzed, 88.2% contained physical aggression, principally spanking, gagging, and slapping, while 48.7% of scenes contained verbal aggression, primarily name-calling. Perpetrators of aggression were usually male, whereas targets of aggression were overwhelmingly female.

A Google search for "bestiality" generated 2.7 million returns.

It's probably not unrealistic to say that porn makes up some 30% of the total data transferred across the internet.[103]

Mankind has always found ways to record sexual experience, as can be witnessed by the earliest cave drawings.[104] And humanity has also used every technological step forward to portray the sex act – from early paint, ink, paper, photography, and video to the internet.

The Victorians, spurred in no small part by the erotic art discoveries of Pompeii, invented the concept of pornography by policing erotic imagery and cordoning it off. In fact, the word "pornography" did not enter the English language as the familiar word it is now until 1857.

Pornography was created by putting the sex out of sight, and it has been "recreated" by the internet, which is putting it very much "back in sight", as the figures demonstrate. In fact, in another example of "transformative reshaping", sexual acts are almost as back in sight as they were in Pompeii, where, in a pre-Victorian society they were considered acceptable, if not de rigeur. In fact Romans, rather than consider images of the sexual act "pornographic" and hide them away, usually associated them with luxury, pleasure, and high status.[105]

But unlike the Pompeian images, which were a natural part of Roman life, this transformative reshaping has burst into the public domain in a sudden and unpoliced way, provoking an important debate about the prevalence and effect it is having. Attempts to censor and control to protect the young[106] are already in motion, but even in the days of the sealed magazine on the top shelf, there was always an access route for the intrepid desperados.

And for the obsessive, internet sex can have a disturbing effect on psychological functioning, in some ways analogous to the impact of a psychoactive substance such as drugs or alcohol. Experts are seeing a marked increase in people presenting with these apparently addictive sexual behaviours. And there is every reason to think this will become more of a problem rather than less as use of the internet and online sexual materials become even more widespread.[107]

All these issues will soon be challenged and assessed even further as internet-enabled technology explodes sex out of the 2D screen and into the realm of augmented and virtual reality.

A site called Red Light Center has up to two million users. It's a massive multiplayer online reality (an MMO), like Second Life or World Of Warcraft, only with blaring hair-rock, a 1990s Vegas vibe and, of course, sex. It is pretty crude on first examination, but is clearly working for the many people who have signed up for an online presence. Red Light Center works on a freemium model: you can wander around for free, chatting to other users, or dancing in the nightclub (not advised). But if you want to be able to get your kit off and your libido on and up, you need to pay for VIP membership. It also has an internal economy with its own currency, "Rays," which have a (pretty stable) real-world exchange value. Real and virtual goods and services are for sale. There's a Camgirl Alley, where you can steer your avatar for interactive pornography. You can buy clothes, shoes, and imaginary property. And if you can't persuade another player to sleep with you, there are others who will have avatar sex with you for Rays.

"There are professional working girls and some of them make quite a good living," says Brian Shuster, CEO of the Red Light Center's parent company, Utherverse. "Even if you're only charging two or three dollars a time for virtual sex, that can quite quickly add up." These working girls pay rent to Utherverse for a place in the virtual bordello.

Indiana University professor Bryant Paul believes that, "We really are on the cusp of being able to have virtual sex that is damn close to the real thing. If you look at interactive sex technology, there's a triple-A engine: affordability, accessibility, and anonymity. Add to that that it augments what's possible: you can get more pleasure, more vibration, more thrust. A person who has a five-inch penis can operate a ten-inch teledildonic device and see what that does to a person. So that augmentation issue is very important: it offers the opportunity to improve, to augment the type of sex that people are having."

He adds, "I've yet to meet a person that can vibrate at 120hz. And there's something to be said for that, you know? That the technology is potentially able to offer a level of pleasure that is higher than the real thing. That's going to have real ramifications for what people expect."[108]

Such technology is appearing. And fast. As I mentioned in the previous chapter, hardware development is increasing at an exponential rate to match the growing desire for interconnectivity and the Internet of Things. Again, the porn industry is on the curve, if not ahead of it.

TELEDILDONICS HAVE ARRIVED

 Teledildonics (also known as "cyberdildonics") is real or fictional technology for remote sex (or, at least, remote mutual masturbation), where tactile sensations are communicated over a data link between the participants.

The hardware is no better evidenced than by taking a look at start-up Kiiroo. Kiiroo makes OPue, a vibrating dildo equipped with sensors that remotely stimulate and the SVir, a male masturbator that's like an intelligent, reactive "fleshlight". So, a girl fondles her OPue and a guy gets similarly fondled by his SVir. Apparently, these will also sync up to the action in adult films. Kiiroo is just attempting to take flight, but this is no doubt an example of companies at the vanguard of this kind of physical-meets-virtual recreation.

I chose the porn industry to begin this chapter because it reveals a number of formative forces that will reshape our leisure time. Prevalence and ease of connection puts access to things we like to do literally at our fingertips.

Now we can have sex without having sex.

Heightened experience through augmented and virtual reality will place us in multisensory places that we can enter more often and more freely than ever before, blurring again the lines between working, resting, and playing.

PLAYING BIG GAMES

 For example, the global online games market (including video game console hardware and software, online, mobile, and PC games) is nearly a $100 billion business. It's bigger than the movie industry and the launch of a new game is accorded as much, if not more, significance than the launch of a major new movie.

An entire recreational industry of some stature has grown up with the internet, challenging, entrancing, and training successive generations of online gamers that span a wide age group depending on the type and complexity of the game. "No other sector has experienced the same explosive growth as the computer and video game industry," says Michael D. Gallagher, president and CEO of the Entertainment Software Association. "Our creative publishers and talented workforce continue to accelerate advancement and pioneer new products that push boundaries and unlock entertainment experiences. These innovations in turn drive enhanced player connectivity, fuel demand for products, and encourage the progression of an expanding and diversified consumer base."[109]

And the demographics may surprise us: the gender split in game-playing is 53% male and 47% female, and 29% of gamers are over the age of 50 (helped possibly by the trend of "game communities" for older players).

And gamers have grown up to have "gamer kids" and families are gaming together, though there remains room for growth: more than one-third of parents play games with their kids regularly (at least once a week) and more than half play at least once a month. Sixteen per cent of kids play with parents, 40% play with friends, 17% play with a spouse or significant other, and 34% play with other family members.[110]

In less than a generation, video games have morphed from a cult diversion into a mass medium. This mass of gamers will be able to dip in and out of their games with effortless fluidity.

"As mobile devices (smartphones and tablets) continue to grow, the mobile game category will show the biggest growth due to the entertainment value provided by games compared with other app categories," said Brian Blau, research director at Gartner. "This growth is fuelled by healthy premium mobile device sales globally and a desire by consumers to play games on these multifunction devices that are capable of displaying increasingly sophisticated game content."[111]

The notion of "playtime" is no longer a segregated concept. Playing with your friends over lunch, coffee, or even at your desk is now a fact of life. Of the people surveyed by salary.com in 2012, 64% said they visit non-work-related websites every day during work hours.[112]

Equally pervasive is online gambling. About 51% of the world's population takes part in some form of gambling every year. And the explosive effect of the internet has turned this into a huge, growing, money-spinning enterprise. In fact, online gambling has proven to be the biggest phenomenon in recent years, with a net worth in excess of $30 billion. In 2012 it expanded at the rate of 2.5%. The games that dominate are wagering, casino, and poker.[113]

> Anything and everything we want to see, play with and enjoy is now with us 100% of the time.

Pornography, video games, gambling – all these "recreational" activities have grown through prevalence and ease of connection to become expressions of leisure that coexist with other daily functions, such as work and rest.

At the opening of this chapter I touched upon the growing desire for global interconnectivity and looked at plans that Google and Facebook had to bring universal internet to the planet.

This heralds probably the biggest shift in leisure activity of all. The provision of the internet, per se, is already opening the door to a significant and paradigm-shifting way in which we consume television and film.

The previous chapter remarked upon the arrival of new technology (Blockchain) that would fundamentally change our perspective on viewing TV and film. The market is now wide open for devices to stream content directly to any device you choose. The big players have fired the starting gun. Sony, Amazon, Roku, Xbox,[114] Google, and Apple are all selling internet-enabled devices to provide the content you require.

It's early days, but there is no doubt that a fundamental shift is taking place. Once we believed it was the television set or radio that provided the entertainment. They were warm, glowing, comforting objects fixed in the corner of our lounges. Now, like all internet leisure, the entertainment that was provided by TV and Radio has exploded into the many devices we utilize throughout the day.

TV stations that broadcast to us are now less relevant than individually packaged content. News, weather, and sports updates have already migrated to our mobile phones.

The point is this. We operate in a screen-driven world. We are screenagers.[115] We want to watch, say, *True Detective*, whenever and wherever we want, via whichever screen we deem most appropriate. The idea that we might have to stay in one fixed place to view it at a certain time is anathema to a generation weaned on an internet diet of "whatever you want – now." We are "cutting the cord" on our dependency on the box in the corner of the room. And mobile is taking a bigger share.

Mobile video traffic exceeded 50% of total mobile data traffic by the end of 2012 and grew to 55% by the end of 2014, according to Cisco.[116] This rings the death knell of not only channel-controlled viewing, but also cable and satellite providers. It is these two businesses that make up what we might call the TV industry.

The TV itself is not under threat. It remains a primary viewing platform and probably will remain so for some time. But television stations and cable providers are having to package their prime content and make it available on multiple devices.

"Broadcasting" is a slowly dying industry. It has been replaced by the internet, which has analyzed and fractionalized its content and spread it out over a plethora of internet-enabled devices.

With the explosion of smartphones and digital tablets and the steady rise of internet-connected televisions and gaming consoles, consumers are increasingly watching streaming content or downloading video when and where they want. As of October 2013, 48% of all US adults and 67% of those under the age of 35 watched streamed or downloaded video during a typical week, up from 45% and 64%, respectively, just six months earlier. At the same time, the share of households considered "cord-cutters" – those with high-speed internet, but no cable or satellite TV – is on the rise, especially among video streamers.[117]

> Broadcasting is a slowly dying industry. Producing and Providing for internet-enabled devices satisfies the requirement of the upgraded consumer.

And that number gets even higher if you look at a younger segment of the population. Almost a quarter of young adults between 18 and 34 who subscribe to Netflix or Hulu don't pay for TV, Experian found. "The young millennials who are just getting started on their own may never pay for television," said John Fetto, a senior analyst at Experian Marketing Services. "Pay TV is definitely declining."[118]

This stark chart of US cable subscribers tells the tale clearly (see *Figure 21* over the page).

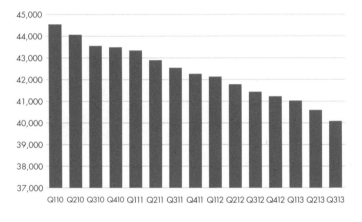

GOODBYE, CABLE TV

■ CABLE VIDEO SUBSCRIBERS

FIGURE 21: THE INTERNET HAS CHANGED THE WAY WE WATCH TELEVISION. MORE CONSUMERS THAN EVER ARE WATCHING STREAMED OR DOWNLOADED PROGRAMS WHEN AND WHERE THEY'D LIKE, ON WHATEVER DEVICE THEY'D LIKE.

The future of content-driven programs lies with the big content owner-producers (for example, Disney, Time Warner, BBC), the internet-enabled device content re-sellers (Hulu, Netflix, and Amazon Prime), and the providers of internet-enabled streaming (Sony, Amazon, Roku, Xbox, Google, and Apple).

Our leisure will be with us all the time (see *Figure 22).*

THIS IS ALL WE NEED

FIGURE 22: WHEREVER WE ARE, WE CAN WATCH THE VIDEO AND STREAMING CONTENT OF OUR CHOICE, ON OUR OWN DEVICE.

The idea that rest and relaxation is somehow an enforced relief period from work is no longer a paradigm that holds much authority. Cult leisure activities have entered the mainstream as they have become more accessible, and we are now able to assimilate new cultures and behaviours into our lives faster than ever before.

Social media is now a big driver of common knowledge and acceptance, bringing worldwide, shareable content to a massive market. The artist Psy's "Gangnam Style" video has now reached more than two billion views, whereas it is entirely conceivable he may have never been heard of, outside his native South Korea, some ten years ago. As of November 2015, eleven music videos have received more than one billion views.

Homo sapiens is now irreversibly open to every niche leisure pursuit, whenever and however they choose. We have upgraded the way we access our leisure. In fact leisure is interwoven into our daily routine making it permanently available rather than segmented into specific times.

IT'S ALL RELATIVES

WE ARE OMNIPOTENT DATA PACKAGES.
WE ARE IMMORTAL.

 Human beings are able to store within themselves a phenomenal amount of data. A certain Yevgeniy Grigoryev calculates the amount to be 150 zettabytes, or 75 billion fully loaded 16gb iPads.[119] We are data because we can convert our thoughts, actions, and desires into a digital format. And now we are interacting with other data from many different sources on an exponential level. Some of these interactions we know about. Others we don't.

Every day we are transmitting packages of our data through internet channels. But it's not a simple transmission. It is received, transmitted, processed, reprocessed, filtered, connected, reconnected, aggregated, matched, and stored (actions that are just the tip of the "connectivity iceberg") at an astonishing rate. And the motives for our data donation change minute by minute. We give it away for free, for commercial use and for reward, as we are now aware that our data connects and reconnects with other data that is useful to both sender and receiver.

What we watch, where we live, where we go, what we buy, who we talk to, and what we search all become forms of stored and retransmitted data.

Broadly speaking, this stored data is either "structured" (such as point-of-sale data when your credit card or loyalty card is swiped, census data, zip codes, or GPS data) or "unstructured" (like social chat, e-mails, videos, and photos). Human-to-human contact, connection, and correspondence are clearly more about data-to-data flow as they are a flesh-to-flesh handshake, or eye-to-eye contact.

In fact, our data is erupting from our devices and being propelled forward, analyzed, attended to, and responded to so fast, efficiently, and effectively that we are actually communicating even when we think we are not. In fact, we communicate widely when we are alone, asleep, or even dead.

Our digital afterlife is raising many issues, not the least of which, of course, is ethical. Having access to a loved-one's digital life or having to deal with continued responses to someone who has passed away recognizes the fact that our data is immortal, even when we are not.[120]

DAVID BOWIE AND IMMORTALITY

 In turning his death into an art piece, the artist David Bowie was able to say a lot within the close confines of creativity. Among the many messages he sent, one clearly chimes with the aspirations of Zuckerberg, Page, and Brin.

In "Lazarus," with buttons, like pennies for the ferryman, on his eyes, he sings: "Everybody knows me now."

Google's Project Loon[121] (I fancy Bowie might have liked that moniker) and Facebook's Internet Satellite programme aim to bring internet access to the remaining majority of the world that does not have it. "We're going to keep working to connect the entire world – even if that means looking beyond our planet," Mark Zuckerberg said in a Facebook post.

One day soon, one of the big platforms will be able to speak to the entire world at the same time. Who will say "Hello world" first?

Bowie's death was announced on his social media accounts and his son confirmed it on Twitter. With phenomenal speed it seemed like everyone knew of his death. Twitter exploded with some 4.3 million Tweets about his death in the first seven hours after the event. Exactly how many knew by the end of the initial 24-hour news blitz is difficult to say. Certainly everyone with internet access knew.

By the end of 2015, there were approximately 3.4 billion internet users, representing some 46% of the world's population.[122]

I think you could safely round that figure up to a neat 50% if you add those who don't have internet access but know someone who does.

In a very short period of time, more than 3.5 billion people could have known that Bowie had died via one of their interconnected devices. That leaves, possibly, just over 3.5 billion people who didn't hear the news and don't know he's dead. Possibly.

As we have seen, anything in billions is a small figure in the scheme of modern connectivity. Billions were way too small, for example, to measure the number of music streams tracked by Next Big Sound in the first half of 2015. The music analytics company says it tracked a gigantic 1.03 trillion music streams from a host of popular streaming services. Bowie's domination of the current charts ensures he will be playing a part in keeping those figures well into the trillions.

It is estimated that 6.4 billion connected "things" will be in use in this year (up 30% from 2015).[123] Assigning just one paltry transaction per day between these devices, we are looking at an annualized minimum of 2.3 trillion moments of connectivity. Some of these trillions will be brand new moments of connectivity to add to the 11 trillion messages sent and received on WhatsApp last year.

Bowie stage-managed both his life and his death. His demise was part art, part music, part wake, and part stunt. Wonderfully wonderful and cruelly wonderful at the same time.

And in doing so, he played into the exponential possibilities of cyberspace. At his final moment, he upgraded himself and revealed to many billions the awesome abilities we now we have. His sad but masterful gift will have generated trillions of bits of interconnected, retweeted, rehashed comments.

Uploading our final moments as we unplug from life is within the reach of all of us. Staying alive forever among the billions of people and trillions of chats in cyberspace is a reality that Bowie hints at; after all, Lazarus returns to life just a few days after his death.

We can manipulate our data. "Digital Cosmetic Surgery" allows us to be whoever we want to be. And we can have multiple personalities, too. There can be many versions of ourselves roaming the internet, meeting people, conversing, and asking for connectivity.

What I'm *not* referring to here is dissociative identity disorder, (formerly referred to as multiple personality disorder), which is a severe psychological condition. Those who suffer from this can expect an identity that is fragmented into two or more distinct personalities. Although it is becoming clear that we are getting close to blurring the edges in the distinction between dissociative identity disorder and distorting our personalities online.

> We can send as many versions of ourselves into cyberspace as we wish. True versions, Possible versions, Real versions, Quantified versions, even Dead versions.

Susan Greenberg marshals a strong force of research to demonstrate that social networks allow us to deliberately construct "a socially desirable self to which individuals aspire but have not yet been able to achieve."[124]

A "possible self" can be displayed to sit alongside the "true self" (expressed in anonymous environments without the constraints of social pressures) and the "real self" (the conformed individual who is restricted by social norms in face-to face-interventions).[125]

All three "selves" – possible, true, and real – can now be quantified. The quantified self sits online in devices, measuring and assessing our objectives and achievements across a range of inputs–food consumed, quality of surrounding air, sleep patterns, state of arousal, mood, blood oxygen levels, glucose levels, calories ingested, distance walked or jogged, mental performance and, of course, physical performance.

Pew Research Centre calculates that 21% of those of us who track our health or the health of others use technology.[126]

Again, as we have seen, the quantified-self movement has spawned the growth in manufacturing many devices to analyze our human data and feed it back. In 2013, Gartner estimated that the "wearable electronics market with products for the quantified self"[127] would hit $5 billion by the end of 2016. Market estimations that cover all aspects of the quantified self are rare, but simple extrapolations from the number of apps available (thousands) suggest it is enormous and growing.

WE CAN COMMUNICATE WITHOUT COMMUNICATING

>>> We are faced with an extraordinary progression of a natural process – communication. We are animals that can communicate to many people (groups of people and institutions), we can communicate when we are not physically communicating, and we can communicate different versions of ourselves according to who we want to impress, dupe, or be real to. As such, our data transmissions push us way further up the evolutionary scale in a way that our nearest animal cousins could never, ever achieve. It's too early to say where this development will ultimately take us and what the impact will be on our species on a social and emotional level. But one thing is certain, it's a significant progression and will have significant consequences.

We may marvel at dolphins' pulsed sounds and whistles forming a mostly misunderstood sonic language – but we humans are way ahead.

The complex communications system of ants, using pheromones, touch, and sound, is something we love to observe. But in all honesty, its wonder pales into insignificance when compared to how we humans now connect and communicate.

Our data is so personal and valuable that it is protected by law. (In the UK it's the Protection of Data Act 1998) and it has its own protective police force (the Information Commissioner). Other countries have different systems of regulations. In the US, for example, there can be legal detail and differences among states. For example, consider these two 2014 California laws:

The first provides for the "right to be forgotten" online. The other requires websites to disclose whether they honour a user's "do not track" preference.

A ruling from Massachusetts' highest court provides that zip codes may constitute personal information.

Laws are being created and amended to reflect the changing nature of our data and the important recognition that data is every bit as personal as our bodies and minds.

IN FACT, HUMANS ARE "DATA THINGS"

Data is everything, and in data terms we are operating and interacting with machine-to-machine data. Machine-to-machine data is a part of the interactions to be found among the Internet of Things.

We humans are a part of the Internet of Things, because we, too, are a "data thing". Every time you buy from Amazon, your purchase choice becomes a data choice and adds to your own data profile. Then automation kicks in and your data is sent to warehouses or an individual or even a robot to fulfil your order. This transaction is then incorporated into a sophisticated and mechanized feedback loop that advises you on other similar choices. The machines at work, 24 hours a day, 365 days a year, start to learn your profile. They never stop learning.

IDC estimates that by 2020, business transactions on the internet (business-to-business and business-to-consumer) will reach 450 billion per day.[128] In essence, what this means is that a phenomenal amount of business is being – and will be – done without human hands involved. Again, in commercial developmental terms, this really is a giant leap for mankind.

We are also often communicating in a way that is invisible to ourselves.

The explosive donation of our personal data for invisible use is no better seen than in the rise of online dating.

LOVE AND SEX: ALL IS DATA

Revenue projections show online dating sites continuing to grow rampantly. In 2007, dating sites earned about $1.03 billion in revenue, with that figure expected to grow to $2 billion by 2015. These projections are based on the continued integration of the digital world into everyday life.[129]

The industry has grown exponentially in many Western countries. For instance, one in ten Americans have used an online dating site or mobile dating app; 66% of these users have gone on a date with someone they met through a dating site or app; and 23% have met a spouse or long-term partner through these sites.[130]

When you are dating from the comfort of your own device, on the sofa at home, in bed, at work or wherever, you are using the internet to find a matched set of data to your own. You are profiling a potential partner in an automated way. Apps like Tinder even use location-based services to allow your data to roam and harness someone else's matched data. Your data roams non-stop, looking for compatible data. Tinder now makes a colossal 21 million matches a day. These are digital matches, matches that we can make through digital extension. Such a figure cannot be realized any other way.[131]

Happn[132] takes this one step further. Here's how it works: you register via, say, Facebook Connect, and then specify your partner preferences (i.e., load your data preferences) according to age and gender criteria. You then receive a newsfeed that shows the history of the users that match your criteria. Whenever someone else's "matched data" crosses the path of your matched data, their profile appears on your screen. A simple press of the "like" button sends out a "let's meet?" communication.

You connect with people who you have crossed paths with, who you like but who you have never met and were present in a past history that you can inhabit, just as easily as you can inhabit the present day. It's virtual serendipity. Of course the possibility always exists that you can be duped by false data, or "catfished," a term inspired by the 2010 documentary Catfish, which exposed a real-life duping process. A spinoff, MTV's *Catfish: The TV Show*, features individuals going through the uncertain process of online dating.

The Pew Research Center reported that approximately 54% of online daters have felt that a person they've met through the site or app has "seriously misrepresented themselves in their profile."[133] Other research suggests that both men and women deflate their ages and inflate their salaries.[134]

This can be overcome. Apps like "Love Lab" look to authenticate data as much as possible through more sophisticated algorithms and checks. The more authenticated data about yourself you donate, the more accurately you get matched.

Whether dating apps "work" better than physical dating did in the pre-internet age is an altogether different question. We are on the cusp of being able to analyze robust data to determine, for example, whether marriages last longer if the partners meet first online. The average marriage prior to divorce lasts for 13.6 years, according to Economist data.[135] The first major internet dating website is widely held to be the combination of kiss.com and match.com, in 1994 and 1995 respectively, so this is a maturing market. Relationship longevity data can be, and is now, being scrutinized.

> We can now inhabit someone else's past as easily as we inhabit our own present.

But that is not the point. While on paper we might assume that perfectly matched data makes for a more perfect long-term relationship, it could also permit multiple matched sets, offering an explosion of opportunity, and, potentially, promiscuity, that may not at first have been intended.

Online dating is an important indicator of the way we choose to connect. Its long-term effects will be defined by both continuity of usage and success of purpose.

Earlier I said that I believed that the internet has evolved Homo sapiens in a way that previously only the opposable thumb and speech had done. The opposable thumb is normally associated with Homo habilis, our developmental forerunners. The opposable thumb allowed us to climb trees and hold sticks and throw balls. It allowed females to protect children and get greater access to food. It raised us above other animal life. Speech allowed humans to share knowledge, news, and feelings.

The massive explosion in dating sites is another very clear demonstration of our transformative development. There is no way that other animal life on this planet could find a mate in the sophisticated, automated, long distance, and invisible way that we now can. Simple verbal assertions of feeling limit us geographically. Our use of the internet erased that problem overnight.

So, yes, I'll make the point again: this is yet another giant leap for mankind.

Connecting in this way is clearly one of the many self-evident gifts of the internet. And, obviously, we are more connected through data than ever before. David Hughes, an internet pioneer, predicts some implications of this: "All seven-plus billion humans on this planet will sooner or later be 'connected' to each other and fixed destinations, via the Ubernet (not internet). That can lead to the diminished power over people's lives within nation-states. When every person on this planet can reach and communicate two-way with every other person on this planet, the power of nation-states to control every human inside its geographic boundaries may start to diminish."[136]

Total interconnectedness driven by automation will see a sharp redefinition of the terminology of communication. An experiment in Iceland gives some pointers to what is beginning to emerge.

The Book of Icelanders, an online database of residents and their family trees stretching back 1,200 years, is collating DNA data from Iceland's well-defined and small population.[137] On the one hand, collecting such data is very controlled and useful, but on the other it naturally brings to the surface an often unspoken truth.

With such a small DNA pool, it is highly possible you could end up dating – and, lets be honest, bedding – a near relative. Over time such close interbreeding has the potential to cause genetic problems. Inbreeding results in what is termed "homozygosity" (the state of possessing two identical forms of a particular gene), which can increase the chances of offspring being affected by recessive or deleterious traits.[138] This generally leads to the decreased biological fitness of a population, which is its ability to survive and reproduce.

> Icelanders have upgraded themselves to avoid accidental incest. "Bump the app, before you 'bump' in bed!"

For Iceland, this isn't funny.

So not surprisingly, The Book of Icelanders has spawned a new smartphone app to help Icelanders avoid accidental incest. The app lets users "bump" phones and emits a warning alarm if they are closely related. "Bump the app before you bump in bed," says the catchy, if overt, slogan. The Islendiga-App – "App of Icelanders" – is an idea that may only be possible in Iceland, where most of the population shares descent from a group of 9th-century Viking settlers, and where The Book of Icelanders database holds genealogical details of nearly the entire population.

It is a fascinating window into where personally shared data has already taken us. But it is also an interesting sign of where total interconnectedness could be taking us.

We text, we Skype, we message, we call, we video-conference, and we share personal data at an alarming rate. It is almost impossible to measure how much we now connect. It would be easier to measure how many words are spoken on the planet every day. And these words would be a mere fraction of our total communication.

But while we might have been amazed at the exponential growth of inter-human connectivity, it is what happens when we apply analysis through automation and filters that becomes interesting.

New technology being developed by Royal Holloway University finds "weak signals" behind social media chitchat and builds on them to create a picture of what is really being talked about.[139]

Search engines provide a useful but two-dimensional view of subject matter, whereas we now have the capability to understand the "meaning" behind what we are saying and also detect what the discussions hide through what has been called the "spiral of silence." This describes when individuals are reluctant to voice their opinions on the basis that it may contradict the views of their online peers.[140]

In 1971, Albert Mehrabian published a book, *Silent Messages*, in which he discussed his research on nonverbal communication. The book gave birth to the popular notion that only 7% of our communication is verbal. Tonality, expression, look, and body language all contributed too. Since the publication of his book, there have been many discussions and debates about the veracity of his research, but most commentators still agree that verbal communication remains the smaller percentage of total communication.[141]

Efforts to analyze the "weak signals" in our machine-driven data communication clues are in essence efforts to understand the nonverbal communication inherent in our internet activity.

The reason this data can be analyzed in such a way is because we donate it freely. Tweets, for example, are called "opted-in" data. What that means is you don't just donate freely, you actively opt to donate freely. To anyone, or any machine, anywhere.

This automated data analysis is creating a new form of correspondence. A "push notification" is a message we are sent that is based on information preferences expressed in advance. A customer "subscribes" to various information "channels" provided by a server; whenever new content is available on one of those channels, the server pushes that information out to the customer.

Of course, "pushing out information" is another way of describing communication. When my British Airways app lets me know key information about my flight, it is in essence an automated flight attendant talking to me about what I need to consider next. But this flight attendant can talk personally, and in subtly different ways, to thousands of customers at the same time. We are being spoken to in a personalized, useful, and meaningful way, but not as an individual.

We have developed a mass communication system that recreates the personal touch. But this "person" is in thousands of different places around the world and talks in thousands of different ways. Clever, magical, and not a little eerie.

This kind of individual personalization, when done well, can engage us with, and warm us to, people and organizations we have never met, but with the same sense of delight as a message from a close family member. In some respects, it can make us feel that we are never alone and have a companion by our side.

Push notifications operate well in the domain of mobile technology and remind us that communicating is now not just "messaging" but is companionship. As we are mobile, so too are the connections that we want to have or make. We want our kids' numbers stored in our smartphones, but we also want the airline or retail store to stay personally in touch.

The chart over the page demonstrates how communication has developed over time (see *Figure 23*).

TRANSFORMATION OF COMMUNICATION

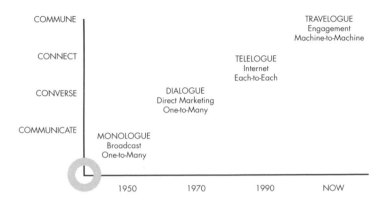

FIGURE 23: THE ENORMOUS CHANGES IN COMMUNICATION OVER THE PAST CENTURY MAKE IT POSSIBLE TO COMMUNICATE WITH ANYONE, AT ANY TIME, FROM WHEREVER WE WANT, AS WELL AS COMMUNICATE WITH MULTIPLE PEOPLE AT ONCE.

We still enjoy receiving information in the way our parents did. We just sit back and allow someone to tell us something. It's easy and for the most part satisfying. The more memorably told, the more likely it will stick. It's good, old-fashioned monologue broadcasting. One message sent out to many people. And it still thrives.

Chile's state broadcaster, TVN, reported that more than a billion people watched the rescue of the trapped miners on television around the world. Millions more watched on live video streams on the internet. Live-streaming service Ustream said it served more streams – 5.3 million –

over the course of the rescue than during any one previous event. The previous record holders were US President Barack Obama's inauguration, at 3.8 million total streams, and the July 2009 memorial service for Michael Jackson, at 4.6 million.

But consider this. The YouTube user PewDiePie has reached over 37 million subscribers and, as of June 2015, his channel has received more than 9 billion video views. He too is a broadcaster. He is such a successful broadcaster that the Swedish newspaper *Expressen* estimated that PewDiePie earned at least $7 million in 2014.[142] "He appeals to an attractive demographic of teens and young adults," said Ian Maude from Enders Analysis. "It's strange to imagine that somebody can earn so much from YouTube, but the equivalent of half the UK is watching his videos."[143]

PewDiePie's revenues come from advertising and, as such, he operates exactly like any commercial TV station.

Dialogue-based communication (or conversation) is also thriving, with telemarketing techniques morphing into online chat with, say, your bank and, of course, e-commerce.

Direct marketing is growing[144] as technology allows greater personalisation and access to niche products. When we communicate something very specific, something very specific and tailored comes back to us.

> One day we will all be connected. And we could speak to each other in Emoji, aping the pre-alphabet language of Egyptian Pharaohs.

Much has been made of the internet's ability to destroy conventional media, but that is not really happening. It is reshaping it and giving it a different outlet and greater oxygen and light to prosper. As all forms of media prosper, language spreads, propagates, and takes root.

Emoji could well be the world's first global language.[145] Certainly, according to academics, emoji is now the fastest-growing language in the UK and evolving faster than ancient forms of communication, such as hieroglyphics. That claim comes from Professor Vyv Evans of Bangor University who, with telecommunications company Talk Talk, is studying the "speed of evolution" in the use of the little icons instead of words.

"As a visual language, emoji has already far eclipsed hieroglyphics, its ancient Egyptian precursor, which took centuries to develop," he said.

The word emoji literally means "picture" – (e) + "character" (moji) in Japanese. It was added to the Oxford English Dictionary in 2013.

In a breath-taking feat of the use of this new language,

tennis star Andy Murray marked his wedding day last month by tweeting the story of the day entirely in emoji.

Apple has further globalized the language by adding the option of different skin tones to its happy faces.

The Bangor University survey also discovered that 72% of 18- to 25-year-olds said they found it easier to put their feelings across in emoji icons than in text.

Feelings, again, are the "weak signals" that give away so much important and valuable information. Feelings are principally emotional. To turn these emotions into easily transmitted and read data is an opportunity to express our feelings simply, quickly, and across a wide plateau of potential recipients.

The very building blocks of communication—language, feelings, weak signals, human, vocal, written, painted, musical—have been altered as they have become data.

Work undertaken by Oxford Professor Robin Dunbar (giving rise to the theory of "Dunbar's Number") puts a maximum number on this and suggests a cognitive limit to the number of people with whom one can maintain stable social relationships. These are relationships in which an individual knows who each person is and how each person relates to every other person. He puts the figure at 150. Not that this figure is a barrier for pop star Shakira, who has in excess of 100 million "likes" on her Facebook page.

A friend used to be an individual with whom one had a bond of affection. Clearly for many a friend is now a contact, a reference point linked by data transmission.

And as such, a piece of music is a shared file.

A simple emotion can be easily expressed as a symbol.

A desire can be packaged and sent round the world in an instant.

We stand at the beginning of a new chapter of multidimensional, inter-human communication. These dimensions will be part vocal, part gestural, part natural, part digital, part actual, part virtual, part real, and part robot.

HUMAN, UPGRADE THYSELF!

Among all the massive demobilisation, repatriating, and restructuring of humankind that began in the final months of 1945, there was time and talent for the countries that founded the United Nations to turn their minds to the improvement of the world's population. A well-deserved and long overdue "upgrade", if you like.

What they proposed was a kind of global enhancement for mankind–a gift no doubt sponsored by the fact that mankind had degraded and downgraded itself over the previous six (or maybe even thirty) years.

The UN moved fast.

In fact, in less than four months, from July to November 1946, two organizations were created that were to upgrade the lives of billions of people by emphasising the importance of, and "right of access" to, health and education.

The vision was noble and bold. Everyone had a right to education and everyone should be able to reach the highest standard of health (see *Figure 24*).

Everyone has the right to education
All must attain the highest possible level of health

FIGURE 24: IN 1946, THE UNITED NATIONS DECLARED THAT EVERYONE HAD THE RIGHT OF ACCESS TO EDUCATION AND HEALTH.

The constitution of the World Health Organization (WHO) was signed by all 51 countries of the United Nations, and by 10 other countries, on July 22 1946. On November 4 1946, UNESCO[147] came in to force, with a constitution expressing a belief "in full and equal opportunities for education for all."

Since that time, it has been part of UNESCO's mandate to make those opportunities a reality. Several legally binding instruments enshrine education as a right, beginning with the 1948 Universal Declaration of Human Rights, which states, "Everyone has the right to education"(Article 26).

WHO's constitution states that its objective "is the attainment by all people of the highest possible level of health."[148] This objective is updated fairly regularly with the latest iteration stating:

"Health is a state of complete physical, mental, and social wellbeing and not merely the absence of disease or infirmity.

The enjoyment of the highest attainable standard of health is one of the fundamental rights of every human being without distinction of race, religion, political belief, economic, or social condition.[149]

The health of all peoples is fundamental to the attainment of peace and security and is dependent upon the fullest cooperation of individuals and states."

We might in today's parlance describe this big WHO agenda and the UNESCO charter as "global wellbeing," and, broadly speaking, they are doing a good job.[150]

Globally, the number of deaths of children under five years of age fell from 12.7 million in 1990 to 6.3 million in 2013. In developing countries, the percentage of underweight children under five years old dropped from 28% in 1990 to 17% in 2013. Globally, new HIV infections declined by 38% between 2001 and 2013. Existing cases of tuberculosis are declining, along with deaths among HIV-negative tuberculosis cases.

In 2010, the world met the United Nations Millennium Development Goals target on access to safe drinking water, as measured by the proxy indicator of access to improved drinking water sources, but more needs to be done to achieve the sanitation target.

And from an educational standpoint, the planet is learning more and attaining more valued and recognized qualifications. Around the globe, more children than ever can go to school and have the opportunity to acquire the skills needed for the workplace, for their community, and for life.[151]

The United Nations was (and still is) powerful and well intentioned. The upgrade is working.

A NEW FORCE IS UNITING NATIONS

 But of course the entity that is uniting the nations today is an altogether different power. The internet has no grand strategies. It just has myriad facilitations instead.

Human enhancement is one such facilitation. The internet has created a new environment for the furtherance of learning, and a new ability to manage health. Working independently and often unaware of the statutes, governances, and codes of the UN, the internet has accelerated the UN's programme at an unimaginable speed and across the widest possible strata of society.

The speed and spread of growth in learning and health is delivered, as we would by now expect, in an altogether very different way, so that significantly upgrading what we know and improving our wellbeing are now well within our grasp.

But there is a catch.

Evidence is emerging that far-reaching access to the internet and super-fast broadband speeds are not by themselves enough to help us improve ourselves. It is our ability to skilfully harness our newly discovered "exponential opposable thumb" that will be the measure of our potential to extend ourselves to do more than we ever thought possible (see *Figure 25*).

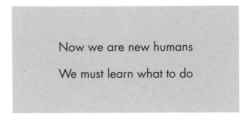

Now we are new humans

We must learn what to do

FIGURE 25: THE EXPLOSION OF THE INTERNET MEANS WE HAVE TO UPGRADE OUR SKILL SETS.

A September 2015 OECD[152] study concluded: "As long as computers and the internet have a central role in our personal and professional lives, students who have not acquired basic skills in reading, writing, and navigating through a digital landscape will find themselves dangerously disconnected from the economic, social, and cultural life around them."

The study looked at computer use among 15-year-olds across 31 nations and regions, and found that students who used computers more at school had both lower reading and lower math scores, as measured by PISA.[153] The study, published September 15 2015, was actually conducted back in 2012, when the average student across the world, for example, was using the internet once a week, doing software drills once a month, and e-mailing once a month. But the highest-performing students were using computers in the classroom less than that.

> We are upgraded humans, but we don't always know what to do with our new skills.

"Those that use the internet every day do the worst," says Andreas Schleicher, OECD director for education and skills, and author of "Students, Computers and Learning: Making the Connection," the OECD's first report to look at the digital skills of students around the world. The study was controlled for income and race; between two similar students, the one who used computers more generally scored worse.

Home computer use, by contrast, wasn't as harmful to academic achievement. Many students in many high-performing nations reported spending between one and two hours a day on a computer outside of school. Across the 31 nations and regions, the average 15-year-old spent more than two hours a day on the computer.

To upgrade ourselves, we must learn a new skillset. Like learning to walk or talk, our internet skills come through a series of failed attempts and utterances. We get bruised and misunderstood. We are crawling through the internet right now and babbling, often nonsensically, our way through the plethora of communication outlets. But one thing we do know is that we will soon become adept and eloquent in all manner of ways. Once we can walk, we can run, and once we can talk we can craft our social and cultural lives.

In both education and wellbeing, there are some interesting, albeit unproven, early shoots of global self-improvement, facilitated by the internet.

UPSIDE-DOWN LEARNING

 Pre-internet education, worldwide, was based on a "one-to-many" monologue broadcast system. Children at school were placed "in loco parentis", allowing the educational establishment organization to take on some of the functions and responsibilities of a parent. The teacher and the textbook were 100% correct at all times and many subjects were, at some point, "taught by rote", which is essentially learning by chanting. Many countries still adopt this method.

A country's culture is most often the starting point of educational learning (and to a great extent it still is), so that in France you might know who Vercingetorix is, or who broke the Soissons Vase (it was Clovis, of course). But in Britain, just a few miles away, you'll know who William the Conqueror is, and which King burnt the cakes (Alfred, of course).[154] But at the university level, there is a greater degree of standardization of content and delivery. In fact, the "European University" is now the model for universities globally. Since the first university opened its doors in Bologna in 1088, the tone and style of higher education hasn't really changed. At university, tradition and status quo are considered a good thing. Being older means being wiser and knowing more.

Leading expert on the development of the university, Professor Walter Rüegg, in his *History of the University in Europe*, writes, "No other European institution has spread over the entire world in the way in which the traditional form of the European university has done. The degrees awarded by European universities – the bachelor's degree, the licentiate, the master's degree, and the doctorate – have been adopted in the most diverse societies throughout the world."[155]

For hundreds of years, the same basic principles of education have been adhered to.

I teach. You learn. An independent assessor examines you. You are graded, from various degrees of success down to fail.

While governments spent the post-war years measuring, introducing, and withdrawing curriculum policies and egalitarian standards, in truth not much happened in the world of education until, very quietly, two years after the internet appeared, a nascent concept was introduced that would have the potential to turn global education on its head. In 1993, Alison King wrote a paper[156] that fired the starting gun for what was to be a new internet-based method of teaching and learning. The paper, "From Sage on the Stage to Guide on the Side," proposed that information transmission be taken out of the classroom and put into the home. Classroom time, she asserted, should be kept for constructing meaning from information. In essence, homework would be done at school and schoolwork would be done at home.

Eighteen years later, Clintondale High School in Michigan (a school ranked among the worst 5% in the state, with a 52% failure rate in English, 44% failure rate in math, and 41% in science), tried the experiment. By then the theory was known as "flipped learning" or "the flipped classroom".

The experiment paid off. The English failure rate dropped from 52% to 19%; in math, from 44% to 13%; in science, from 41% to 19%; and in social studies, from 28% to 9%. After 2011 the now "flipped" school's failure rate dropped from 30% to 10%. Graduation rates soared above 90%. College attendance went from 63% in 2010 to 80% in 2012.

Getting information has never been easier. Just about every single fact you want or need to know can be found on the internet, not least from Wikipedia.

WORLD BRAIN

>> Wikipedia would have appealed to author HG Wells who, in a series of talks entitled "World Brain", predated even McLuhan in envisioning the internet. Excited by developments in radio, HG Wells predicted a time when every household in the world would have a radio and would receive educational broadcasts. He went further. He believed that these radios would eventually transmit information, too, and that the hundreds of thousands of broadcasts and transmissions would form a kind of "net" around the planet. He felt this net could provide useful alerts against despotic behaviour and could hold all human knowledge–a kind of "world brain".

Wells then laid out a vision for "a sort of mental clearinghouse for the mind, a depot where knowledge and ideas are received, sorted, summarized, digested, clarified, and compared." Wells felt that technological advances such as microfilm could be used toward this end so that "any student, in any part of the world, will be able to sit with his projector in his own study at his or her convenience to examine any book, any document, in an exact replica."[157]

Wikipedia, YouTube, Twitter, and Google will all answer your immediate questions. Alison King was right to understand that just transmitting information in schools was not a productive way of imparting knowledge.

There have always been concerns that a "digital divide" would preclude some pupils, less economically privileged, from being able to learn online at home, or that broadband access would not be sufficient.

Today, proliferating and strengthening of the internet is beginning to negate these issues fast. Take a look at the table over the page, which lists the top twenty countries that are ranked highest for the best school education. Next to them are countries ranked by best high speed internet.[158] This chart is highly correlational and suggestive but the data is, nonetheless, surprising (see *Figure 26*).

I can hear people right now putting up their hands and shouting, "Yes, but it's all related to a country's wealth. If you can afford the internet infrastructure, you can afford to educate your citizens!"

But that list does not stack up in the same way as the previous one. Look now at the comparison of best school

Rank	Best School Education	Best High Speed Internet
1	South Korea	South Korea
2	Japan	Hong Kong
3	Singapore	Japan
4	Hong Kong	Switzerland
5	Finland	Sweden
6	United Kingdom	Netherlands
7	Canada	Ireland
8	Netherlands	Latvia
9	Ireland	Czech Republic
10	Poland	Singapore
11	Denmark	Finland
12	Germany	United States
13	Russia	Belgium
14	United States	Israel
15	Australia	Norway
16	New Zealand	Romania
17	Israel	Denmark
18	Belgium	United Kingdom
19	Czech Republic	Austria
20	Switzerland	Canada

FIGURE 26: THE HIGHEST-RANKED EDUCATION SYSTEMS AROUND THE GLOBE, COMPARED WITH COUNTRIES WITH THE BEST HIGH-SPEED INTERNET, SHOW LITTLE CORRELATION BETWEEN THE TWO.

education versus GDP.[159] This chart allows us to infer more confidently that simply because a country has the wealth to educate its children does not lead to a better-educated country (see *Figure 27 over page*).

In a March 2015 Pew internet survey among emerging and developing countries, 64% claimed that the increasing use of the internet has been a good influence on education.[160] With access to knowledge via whatever device is at hand, it is clear that the biggest driver of UNESCO's dream will be the internet.

While there are understandable worries about the fast nature of the internet "byte-sizing" what we learn, and while both attention spans and physical development are put under pressure while learning online, the biggest disintermediation must surely be in the physical structure of schools and universities.

MOOCS, or massive open online courses, are taking prestigious teachers out of the physical environment and into the virtual one.

MOOCS aim for unlimited participation and open access. By far the biggest is Coursera, started by two Stanford University professors, Andre Ng and Daphne Koller. By the end of 2015, Coursera had almost 13 million users and is available in twelve languages–English, Spanish, French, Chinese, Arabic, Russian, Portuguese, Turkish, Ukrainian, Hebrew, German, and Italian. The Coursera online

Rank	Best School Education	Highest GDP
1	South Korea	United States
2	Japan	China
3	Singapore	Japan
4	Hong Kong	Germany
5	Finland	United Kingdom
6	United Kingdom	France
7	Canada	Brazil
8	Netherlands	Italy
9	Ireland	India
10	Poland	Russia
11	Denmark	Canada
12	Germany	Australia
13	Russia	South Korea
14	United States	Spain
15	Australia	Mexico
16	New Zealand	Indonesia
17	Israel	Netherlands
18	Belgium	Turkey
19	Czech Republic	Saudi Arabia
20	Switzerland	Switzerland

FIGURE 27: ALTHOUGH IT MAY SEEM THAT WEALTHIER COUNTRIES WITH INTERNET INFRASTRUCTURE WOULD ALSO RANK HIGHLY IN SCHOOL EDUCATION, THEY DON'T CORRELATE.

platform now boasts 1,027 courses from 119 partners, including business schools at the Universities of Michigan and Virginia, IESE Business School in Spain, the Indian School of Business in India, and HEC Paris in France.[161]

Some Coursera courses are free, but the majority are fee-based.

In April 2014, Rick Levin left Yale University as one of the Ivy League's most successful presidents in history and took up his post as CEO of Coursera.

While no one at this stage is seeing an immediate and sudden collapse of the global education market, what is startling about his appointment is that he is an academic of very sound repute.

In his online interview,[162] however, while not revealing the annual revenues of Coursera (surely way in excess of $12 million given the number of paid-for accreditations issued at $49 a pop), he says something revealing.

"About 73% of our learners are outside the US and about half of those are in emerging economies."

Internet-driven education is rapidly moving out from the boundaries of nation states and reaching countries that it has never reached before. And it's not just an education of "general knowledge"; prominent universities are getting involved with MOOCS, making them important and serious.

This too is an example of "reverse networking." Once education was a network we applied for. Now it can also be a single-sourced product that needs access to our network of education-thirsty global citizens.

This network, in 2015, was eagerly looking for courses such as:[163]

- Buddhist Meditation and the Modern World
- NUTR101x: Introduction to Nutrition–Food for Health
- Financial Analysis of Entrepreneurial Ideas
- Hardware Security
- Fundamentals of Management
- Pattern Discovery in Data Mining
- Visual Design
- Foundations of E-Commerce
- The Art of Negotiation
  and
- Algorithms, Biology, and Programming for Beginners

This demonstrates the kind of eclectic mix you would find if there were simply one source for learning.

It is too early to tell what effect MOOCS will have, but if they follow the route of other internet-driven disintermediators, they won't replace, but will simply add, widen, and disrupt.

MOOCS were not created to replace conventional university education in the way video on demand (VOD) was not intended to replace TV. But for sure they will have an impact. October 2015 research from Stanford,[164] suggests that the techniques developed for online learning may lead to great advances in how students learn, both online and in conventional classrooms.

The research clearly brings out the difficulties of sitting both forms of teaching next to each other and comparing. When long-distance students struggle or fail online, teachers find it problematic to jump in and help. In fact, any form of human intervention is bedevilled by the nature of the online access.

Such comparisons will invite disappointments. MOOCS are an early digital species of Alison King's upside-down learning. But despite the disappointments, Professor Mitchell Stevens of Stanford outlined the scope for optimism: "We're looking at a future of lifelong education online. Much of that will come at little or no cost to learners. How can that be a bad thing?"

And that is indeed the point. We don't need to see the courses taken and passed as an indication of success. The success for humans now and forever is that all learning is available at the flexing of a finger. All learning exists. All knowledge is lodged "out there". Education is now no longer encased within a place to go to. It is an asset to draw down whenever we wish.

BEING WELL

 The OECD's (Organisation for Economic Co-operation and Development) monumental work, "How Was Life? Global Wellbeing since 1820",[165] concludes positively that progress in wellbeing has been widespread since the early 20th century, with the possible exception of Sub-Saharan Africa.

But balance this against Gallup's Wellbeing Index,[166] which demonstrates what we might already know: that for the majority of us, improving our wellbeing is not a finite game. Everything in our lives can be improved all the time.

Panama has the highest overall wellbeing in the world. The new report, "2014 Country Wellbeing Rankings Report",[167] ranks 145 countries and areas based on the percentages of their residents that are thriving in three or more wellbeing elements.

The Americas have a strong presence in the ten countries with the world's highest overall wellbeing, with seven countries on the list. After Panama, rounding out the top ten are Costa Rica, Puerto Rico, Switzerland, Belize, Chile, Denmark, Guatemala, Austria, and Mexico.

The five countries with the lowest levels of wellbeing are Tunisia, Togo, Cameroon, Bhutan, and Afghanistan. In fact, in Afghanistan, no residents are thriving in three or more wellbeing elements, and none are thriving in "purpose", "social", or "financial wellbeing".

Globally, higher wellbeing has been associated with outcomes indicative of stability and resilience – for example, healthcare utilization, intent to migrate, trust in elections and local institutions, daily stress, food and shelter security, volunteerism, and willingness to help others.

The internet currently facilitates all of these and a May 12 2010 report by British researchers from the UK's Chartered Institute of IT (known as BCS)[168] found a link between internet access and wellbeing. But some benefit more than others from tapping into the information superhighway, including those with lower incomes or fewer qualifications, people living in the developing world and, perhaps most surprisingly, women.

Overall, the study found that access to the internet leads people to feel better about their lives. "Put simply, people with IT access are more satisfied with life even when taking income into account," said Michael Willmott, the social scientist who authored the study. "Our analysis suggests that IT has an enabling and empowering role in people's lives, by increasing their sense of freedom and control, which has a positive impact on wellbeing or happiness."

A November 2015 report looking at the practice of medicine and public health supported by mobile devices (known by the abbreviation mHealth) forecast that the mHealth solutions market is poised to reach $59.15 billion by 2020, growing at a CAGR (Compound Annual Growth Rate) of 33.4% during the forecast period of 2015 to 2020.

It's true! Access to the internet makes you feel better.

The mHealth solutions market growth can be attributed, the report states, "to the increasing penetration of smart gadgets, increasing utilization of connected medical devices and mHealth apps in the management of chronic diseases, rising healthcare costs creating a need for more affordable treatment options, robust penetration of 3G and 4G networks to provide uninterrupted healthcare services, and rising focus on patient-centric healthcare."

On the other hand, risk of data theft, stringent regulations by the FDA and EU, low guidance from physicians in selecting apps, and resistance from traditional healthcare providers are currently restricting mHealth solutions market growth.

mHealth apps are also hard to find on Android and Apple stores, which to a certain extent presents another major factor slowing the growth of the mHealth solutions market. These restrictions will change and the market is sure to develop the way the study suggests.

A 2015 UN Volunteering Report[169] states that, "Technology is a powerful tool for civic engagement" and that it needs to be developed globally in a way that allows for its inclusive potential to be realized.

The report confirms that the internet is enhancing the speed, breadth, and diversity of volunteering engagement opportunities, whether online or in person, to address local, national, and global issues.[170]

USAGE AND ABUSAGE

 We can upgrade ourselves. We can know more, we can improve our health, and we can connect in a fabulous way. But we can only do this by knowing how to do it.

Managing the speed of growth of the internet requires new physical and mental skills similar to that of other explorers. We need bravery, competence, dexterity, and experience. We need to plan what we are roughly looking for. We need to know what to do with the things we will find. We need to know who to ask.

By asking Google everything, we invest it with a supreme power. We make it our leader. "Who, what, why, where, when, and how" begin our engagement with Google. We have yet to grasp the realization that this leader isn't leading us anywhere, isn't human and is visible only by its utterances, like the oracles of old.

The sudden demise of Google would create confusion, rather than engender mourning, because it fails to connect – yet – on an emotional level.

We can use the internet to grow as a species and we can abuse the internet, too. It holds no view and makes no moral or ethical judgements.

Not even the law can control the internet.

The "dark net" operates an alternative menu of offerings for those so inclined to operate beyond the law, including shielding dissidents, evasion of mass surveillance, enabling computer crime, and the sale of illegal goods or services.

And there is one other essential human upgrade we have to learn as we explore the benefits that come thick and fast:

The Totality of Effect of Constant Dynamic Mutation.

Our everyday lives are substantially different from our everyday lives of ten years ago. That has never happened to us humans before.

Here are my top ten internet-enabled human upgrades

1. The internet is the biggest human creation ever. It will always be the biggest thing we have built, and it will always be bigger than us. Its exponential growth is

beyond the grasp of our current knowledge and will remain that way. All we can do is constantly upgrade.

2. The internet has extended our ability to serve our physical needs. We have huge reach through electronic prostheses that allow us to get what we want, when and how we want it. Distance, availability, terrain, weather–none of these is an obstacle.

3. The internet has created serious, global elders to whom we refer without reverence. Wikipedia, Google, and YouTube answer all our questions. Politicians, priests, and teachers cannot respond in the same way. We have a world brain into which peoples of all nations and many tongues can connect.

4. We can talk to everyone, everywhere, at the same time. We can talk to them as ourselves or as different people. And we can communicate without communicating, letting data automation carry our desires around cyberspace. We can even communicate when we are dead.

5. We can travel wherever we wish and investigate cultures at a minute level. There is just about no place on the planet that we cannot see, be in, or communicate with. We can even be outside the planet. And we can be in all the places we have ever been–all at the same time. All our travel experience can be marshalled into one place if we wish and we can travel back and forth to places as many times a day as we wish.

6. We are now intelligent objects plugged into an intelligent system. We are operational and the system is operational. We are "cooperational", intelligent objects, interdependent and independent of each other at the same time.

7. Sleeping, waking, eating, conversing, entertaining, shopping, dating, learning, celebrating, playing, and relaxing have all become altered states due to the invasive and immersive impact of the internet. The definition of each of the actions can be justifiably altered to demonstrate the impact of DANTI: Data, Automation, New Technologies and the Internet.

8. Our data connects and acts for us as much as our DNA does. Often it is a much more efficient enabler, as in dating. DNA was once communicated through the frail filter of our human characteristics – how we look and speak, for example. Now that we are human data objects and increasingly so, the data of our DNA can be more accurately marshalled for whatever purpose we have in made. Finding an appropriate sexual mate being an obvious one.

9. The internet has upgraded our ability to be commercially astute, so that we now have the same tools as those entities trying to sell to us. But we all have the tools. That's the point. You cannot segment us. We are all screenagers and businesses must now adapt to synchronized mass-marketing and personalization. Everybody is now a potential customer.

10. We are permanently here. For those born within the last twenty years, living online is as natural as breathing. But when we have finally stopped breathing, we can still be around. Nothing of what we have cared for, achieved, lost, or witnessed will ever disappear. (Now, that's what I call an upgrade.)

Every internet development shows that our lives in the next five years will be even more different from our lives today. We are moving at incredible speed, landing in places we did not expect. Landing separately from our colleagues, friends and family who are traveling just as fast but taking a different trajectory. As we travel, and when we land, we change.

We change the way we do things, we change who we say we are, and we change who we actually are. How people actually see us changes and how we connect changes, too. The way we relate to people, the way others relate to us, and the way we prioritize what is important changes.

This human upgrade challenges us emotionally, physically, and psychologically in a way we have never been challenged before.

The speed of the never-ending upgrades to our ever-extending abilities demands that we have to understand that the millions of things we do and think can be radically altered, mutated, enhanced, or erased in an instant.

Reaching out for the "implausibly possible" now coincides with a recognition that we are "constantly repositioning" the present.

Soon we will be able to operate as mature adults in a mature internet age. Soon we will substantially re-sculpt our world, acting together en masse, like the erosive winds that change landscapes forever.

Some of us are well advanced and others are way behind. The difference cannot be defined by gender, race, age, socio-economic background, or country. An "upgrade ability" gap is clearly emerging as the examples in this book have shown.

A pan-human informational programme, delivered in every way possible (physical, virtual, digital) will need to run alongside our lives to educate, inform, and reskill this and future generations.

The existing disciplines dedicated to nurture, advise, and support (schools, college, medicine, psychoanalysis, well-being, and fitness, for example) can find within each other new curricula of human change management.

The prospects are exciting and attainable if the fullest impact of the internet is to be understood.

For the most part, the majority of us blinks wide-eyed in wonder at the myriad starry lights from cyberspace that are coming our way at a phenomenal speed.

ENDNOTES

1. Without which so many "pre-Google" companies would lack the competitive advantage they now need as they add "tech brand" capability to existing software infrastructures and long-established, human-intensive business practices.

2. See *Blockchain*, by Melanie Swan, published by O'Reilly, 2015

3. For a straightforward discussion on this see: Ray Williams, Psychology Today June 30 2014.

4. Rozin, P., & Royzman, E. (2001). "Negativity Bias, Negativity Dominance, and Contagion." Personality and Social Psychology Review, 5, 296-320.

5. Tracy Morgan: The *New York Times* Magazine April 15, 2014

6. The term was originally applied to the financial services industry in 1967. Disintermediation occurred when customers avoided the intermediation of banks by investing directly in bonds and stocks rather than leaving their money in savings accounts. Only in the late 1990s did it become widely popularized.

7. http://enculturation.net/teaching-mcluhan

8. Human development is a massive subject and I make no apology for not spending more time developing such a huge assertion that connects the opposable thumb and the internet. You see, it's an assertion, no more than that. For a wonderfully detailed view of how we have developed see: *The Real Planet of the Apes: A New Story of Human Origins*, by David R Begun, Princeton University Press.

9. Freud. *Civilization and its Discontents* 1961, pp. 38-39.

10. Yes. I am conveniently smuggling a wink into this acronym and inferring a link to Dante Alighieri whose *Divine Comedy* reveals pitfalls and inspiration in his epic journey.

11. When I talk about the internet, I mean the commercial, everyday internet that began to operate in everyday life from early 1992.

12. Cisco Visual Networking Index White paper May 2015.

13. YouTube statistics 2015

14. *Variety* July 2015

15. At 40% per year according to IDC: "The Digital Universe of Opportunities: Rich Data and the Increasing Value of the Internet of Things." April 2014

16. Ibid.

17. As observed at the Interactive Advertising Bureau (IAB) South Africa conference in February 2015.

18. "HM Government a Strong Britain in an Age of Uncertainty : The National Security Strategy" https://www.gov.uk/government/uploads/system/uploads/attachment_data/file/61936/national-security-strategy.pdf

19. Kranzberg, Melvin (1986) "Technology and History: "Kranzberg's Laws," *Technology and Culture*, Vol. 27, No. 3, pp. 544-560.

20. For example: An Android app called BOINC allows smartphone users to contribute their phone's processing power to scientific research.
The app was created by a Berkeley project called BOINC (Berkeley Open Infrastructure for Network Computing), which is known for its computer software that supports more than 50 volunteer computing projects around the world. BOINC software allows projects to tap unused processing power donated by computer owners around the world to analyze data or run simulations that would normally require cost-prohibitive supercomputers.

21. *Nutrition Research and Practice*. Feb 2010; 4(1): 51–57. www.e-nrp.org

22. The level of internet addiction was determined based on the Korean internet addiction self-scale short form for youth, and students were classified as high-risk internet users, potential-risk internet users, and no-risk internet users.

23. *USA Today* March 30 2010

24. See Anne Gibbons, "Food For Thought", *Science Magazine* 2007.

25. https://company.here.com

26. A standard dictionary definition from *The Free Dictionary* by Farlex.

27. Note that a three-minute transatlantic call in 1927 would have cost in the region of $4000 at today's prices.

28. I thank Michael Bayler for opening my eyes to reverse networking. Look online for Michael Bayler's excellent Strategy Review.

29. Note that this has a significant impact on how businesses must segment their audiences. The answer? They mustn't. Those businesses that can talk to the widest breadth of the consumer network will get more customers.

30. In his breakthrough book, *The Theatre and Its Double* (1938), Artaud described theatre as "*la réalité virtuelle.*"

31. A term I first coined in *Implosion*, published by LID, 2013

32. KPCB, May 2015

33. See write-up of the research in: http://www.digitalspy.com/fun/news/a464219/75-percent-of-people-use-their-phone-on-the-toilet.html#~pjPpIhkBSOEIcY

34. According to: Pocket Gamer.biz. Of these apps, games are the largest category (486,568), followed by business (221,574), education (200,369), lifestyle (186,365) and entertainment (136,880).

35. Wireless Application Protocol (WAP) was a technical standard for accessing information over a mobile wireless network. The first company to launch a WAP site was Dutch mobile phone operator Telfort BV in October 1999. In terms of speed, ease of use, appearance, and interoperability, the reality fell far short of expectations when the first handsets became available in 1999. This led to the wide usage of sardonic phrases such as "Worthless Application Protocol."

36. http://www.bloomberg.com/news/articles/2015-04-10/citi-economist-says-it-might-be-time-to-abolish-cash

37. https://bitcoin.org/bitcoin.pdf

38. http://blog.zorinaq.com/?e=66

39. ibid

40. www.weswap.com

41. See: *Daily Telegraph*, http://www.telegraph.co.uk/sponsored/business/sme-home/case-studies/10851312/currency-exchange-weswap.html

42. Other examples are: Kantox, LenInvest, CurrencyFair, Prodigy Finance, FriendsClear, Communitae, TrustBuddy AB, Pret d'Union, RainFin (pty) Ltd., ThinCats, Funding Circle, Orchard Platform, Lending Works, Mintos, Zopa, Lendable,

Lanbay, and Purse, among many others. See: https://dealroom.co/c/weswap_com/similar

43. Key Performance Indicators are used by businesses to measure targets, quality, and success.

44. See www.humanerabrands.com

45. http://timemanagementninja.com/2012/07/5-reasons-you-should-use-headphones-at-work/

46. NSC.org

47. Ohio State University. Research and Innovation Communications. Distracted Walking.

48. Two years after that, in 1912, the Cadillac company released the Model Thirty, "the car with no crank," which was the first production car to feature an electronic self-starter, ignition, and lighting. By dropping the crank starter, Cadillac opened the door to women drivers.

49. See the 2014 Mercedes S Class for more on board tech wizardry.

50. http://www.bodyshopmag.com/News-warranty-direct-repair-duncan-mcclure-fisher.aspx

51. Elon Musk, *CEO* June 12 2014

52. And unmanned freight ships too. See JOC.com "Pondering the realities of unmanned container ships", June 2015.

53. Responsible Travel promotes "responsible tourism." Responsible tourism simply means caring about local communities and culture as well as wildlife conservation and the environment.

54. Sigmo is one of many voice-translating devices requiring internet access via mobile technology http://buysigmo.com.

55. See http://www.globalization101.org

56. World Bank Development Indicators. See also http://www.globalissues.org/article/26/poverty-facts-and-stats#src1

57. Low-cost airlines, increased holiday allowance, greater disposable income (especially among the over-55s), type of holiday ("extreme", "ecological", "winter", etc.), media interest, and online comparison/booking.

58. Vinton "Vint" Gray Cerf is an American internet pioneer, recognized as one of "the fathers of the internet", sharing this title with American engineer Bob Kahn.

59. "Vint Cerf is Taking the Web into Outer Space – Reserve your Mars Address Now," *Wired* magazine Issue 8.01 | Jan 2000

60. Ibid

61. Pew Internet. Life in 2015

62. Ibid

63. Ibid

64. Ibid

65. See: http://www.inition.co.uk/topshop-goes-virtual/

66. See: http://mashable.com/2014/09/18/marriott-oculus/

67. See http://hpi.de/cn/baudisch/projects/scotty.html

68. See: http://www.technologyreview.com/news/525881/what-zuckerberg-sees-in-oculus-rift/

69. For those so inclined to glimpse into the ancients' concept of time, see the stunning poem by the Roman poet Horace: *Diffugere nives*, (Odes IV.7) and/or the AE Houseman translation.

70. Kleiner Perkins Caufield and Byers

71. eMarketer 9/14 (2008-2010), eMarketer 4/15 (2011-2015).

72. For more on Blockchain, see Melanie Swann's book, *Blockchain: Blueprint for a New Economy*. Also, there are plenty of online tutorials.

73. Symantec: Internet Threat Security Report 2014

74. Mandiant Fire/Eye. M-Trends 2015: A View From The Front Lines.

75. Market Investigations Ltd., "Mrs. Housewife and Her Grocer" 1961

76. http://www.geekwire.com/2014/amazon-adds-30-million-customers-past-year/

77. See: http://www.zendesk.com/resources/customer-service-and-lifetime-customer-value

78. http://www.inc.com/aaron-skonnard/why-tech-savvy-ceos-rule-the-world.html

79. http://www.computerworld.com/article/2598707/it-leadership-digital-transformation-needs-a-modern-mission-critical-infrastructure.html

80. TATA Consultancy Services July 2014: The-Road-to-Reimagination-The-State-And-High-Stakes-of-Digital-Initiatives

81. Ibid

82. One of these is surely Turo, a peer-to-peer car rental business. See www.turo.com

83. http://en.wikipedia.org/wiki/Bayes'_theorem

84. "Online Decision-Making" Kevin Askew and Michael D Coovert. Ch. 6 *The Social Net.*

85. http://www.ibeacon.com/8-touchless-mobile-experiences-that-you-can-expect-by-2015/

86. WEAF of New York is credited with airing the first paid radio commercial, on August 28, 1921, for the Queensboro Corporation, advertising an apartment complex. It wasn't until more than 50 years later, in 1973, that the UK heard its first radio commercial, on LBC, for Birds Eye fish fingers.

87. See: The Strange Decline of the Paperboy http://news.bbc.co.uk/1/hi/magazine/7431224.stm

88. More on this in Chapter 5, "Industrious Leisure"

89. See: www.businessinsider.com/how-social-networks-drive-sales-2014

90. See UK Technology Strategy Board https://www.innovateuk.org

91. "Click and collect" has now entered our common purchasing lexicon and as words they aptly define how internet-enabled purchasing is changing the way we shop.

92. Cybernetics is a word coined by group of scientists led by Norbert Wiener and made popular by Wiener's book of 1948, *Cybernetics or Control and Communication in the Animal and the Machine.* The term "cyberspace" began appearing in fiction in the 1980s (for example, the 1980 Vernor Vinge novella *True Names*, and the 1980 John M. Ford novel *Web of Angels*.) Yet it was through the work of cyberpunk science fiction author William Gibson [6] that the word became prominently

identified with online computer networks, beginning with the 1982 story "Burning Chrome" and popularized by his 1984 novel *Neuromancer*.

93. Not least Professor Alessandra Lemma. See *Psychoanalysis in the Technoculture Era* ed. Alessandra Lemma.

94. Professor A Lemma: "Psychoanalysis in Times of Technoculture: Some Reflections on the Fate of the Body in Virtual Space." September 2014.

95. Deleuze, Bergonism 1966.

96. By far the most common usage of the term describes the consumers, enthusiasts who buy products (almost always technical) that fall between professional and consumer-grade standards in quality, complexity, or functionality. *Prosumer* **also commonly refers to those products**. "Prosumer" is a well-accepted category for camcorders, digital cameras, VCRs, "and other video playthings." Higher prosumer expectations lend themselves to increased customizing in Toffler's product-improvement sense.

97. McKinsey Global Institute: Unlocking the Potential of the Internet of Things

98. Over 46% of the global population has internet access according to IWS. But figure masks a more telling statistic. 88% of N America has access and over 73% of Europe. The UK is at 92% and Sweden is 95%. Iceland is over 98%.

99. *Wall Street Journal*, July 1ˢᵗ 2014: "Google Invests in Satellites to Spread Internet Access"

100. See my book *Implosion* pp. 15-19, for more detail on this.

101. Stephen Yagielowicz, "The Internet Really Is Porn"

102. Ibid

103. Ibid

104. Among the oldest surviving examples of erotic depictions are Paleolithic cave paintings and carvings. Some of the more common images are of animals, hunting scenes, and depictions of human genitalia. Nude human beings with exaggerated sexual characteristics are depicted in some Paleolithic paintings and artifacts (e.g., Venus figurines). Recently discovered cave art

at Creswell Crags in England, thought to be more than 12,000 years old, includes some symbols that may be stylized versions of female genitalia. As there is no direct evidence of the use of these objects, it is speculated that they may have been used in religious rituals or for a more direct sexual purpose.

105. See the most informative: "Looking At Lovemaking," by John R Clarke

106. See *New Yorker*, "No Sex Please" 7th October 2013. Prime Minister David Cameron announced a plan to fit every new broadband account in the UK with a "family-friendly" filter. A recent German proposal would have required porn-seekers to verify their age at a public building like a bank or a post office in order to get a PIN code. (It didn't pass.)

107. For excellent contemporary expert comment see: Heather Wood, "The Nature of the Addiction in "Sex Addiction" and Paraphilias," in *Addictive States of Mind*, 2013.

108. The Guardian, Friday June 6 2014

109. The Entertainment and Software Association 2013

110. http://www.bigfishgames.com/blog/2014-global-gaming-stats-whos-playing-what-and-why/

111. Gartner October 29 2013.

112. Salary.com "Wasting Time At Work 2012.

113. Research And Markets. Analyzing The Global Online Gambling Industry 2013.

114. Xbox has an installed based of 76 million already.

115. See *Implosion*, chapter 5

116. Cisco Visual Networking Index: Global Mobile Data Traffic Forecast Update 2014–2019 White Paper

117. Experian Marketing Services: Cross-device video analysis 2014.

118. Ibid.

119. See: http://visual.ly/how-much-data-stored-human-body

120. http://www.ft.com/cms/s/0/7fc0b8e0-4d1c-11e3-9f40-00144feabdc0.html#axzz3e9ePZyG9

121. Balloon-powered internet for everyone. www.google.com/loon/

122. Internet World stats.

123. Gartner, November 10 2015

124. Susan Greenfield, *Mind Change*, pp 120, (2014)

125. Ibid.

126. Pew Center for Research. Jan 27, 2013.

127. Gartner: Market Trends: Enter the Wearable Electronics Market With Products for the Quantified Self. July 2013.

128. http://www.idc.com/

129. http://visualeconomics.creditloan.com/a-business-of-love-online-dating-by-the-numbers/ see also: http://inlinepolicy.com/2014/online-dating-growth-regulation-and-future-challenges/

130. Source: http://www.pewinternet.org/files/old-media/Files/Reports/2013/PIP_Online%20Dating%202013.pdf.

131. Tinder.com

132. www.happn.com

133. http://www.pewinternet.org/2013/10/21/online-dating-relationships/

134. http://visualeconomics.creditloan.com/a-business-of-love-online-dating-by-the-numbers/

135. http://www.economist.com/blogs/graphicdetail/2014/02/daily-chart-10

136. http://www.pewinternet.org/2014/03/11/digital-life-in-2025/

137. Currently around 329,000

138. See: Parental consanguinity and congenital heart malformations in a developing country, Nabulsi, Tamim, Sabbagh, Obeid, Yunis, and Bitar.

139. Groupseer

140. http://www.pewinternet.org/2014/08/26/social-media-and-the-spiral-of-silence/

141. See: http://ubiquity.acm.org/article.cfm?id=2043156

142. *Expressen* newspaper July 7 2015

143. endersanalysis.com

144. See: 5 Main Reasons for Growth in Direct Marketing Activity. http://www.yourarticlelibrary.com/marketing/5-main-reasons-for-growth-in-direct-marketing-activity/13566/

145. http://www.theguardian.com/technology/2014/aug/31/emoji-became-first-global-language

146. For the United States, the rapid demobilization of more than 12 million men and women in the armed service was a major task – not least because almost 8 million of them were still overseas. Operation Magic Carpet repatriated the service personnel from Europe, Asia, and the Pacific. The epic task was completed by the end of 1946.

147. UNESCO, The United Nations Educational, Scientific and Cultural Organization, was founded on November 19 1945.

148. See the Constitution of the Word Health Organization with useful recent updates.

149. Surely today we would add, "gender", "age", and "sexual orientation" to this list.

150. World Health Statistics 2014 contains WHO's annual compilation of health-related data for its 194 Member States, and includes a summary of the progress made toward achieving the health-related Millennium Development Goals (MDGs) and associated targets.

151. OECD Indicators: Education at a Glance 2015

152. OECD oecdeducationtoday.blogspot: "Students, Computers and Learning: Where's the Connection?" Andreas Schleicher

153. Program for International Student Assessment

154. In Australia it would be 1788, Botany Bay, and the colonization, or who was the outlaw who wore the tin hat (Ned Kelly, of course). Interestingly in the United States it would be 9/11 and what happened on July 4 (American Independence, of course!).

155. Rüegg, Walter (1992). *A History of the University in Europe. Vol. 1: Universities in the Middle Ages*. Cambridge University Press. pp. xix–xx.

156. King, Alison. "From Sage on the Stage to Guide on the Side." *College Teaching* 41.1 (1993): pp.30-35.

157. HG Wells. World Brain 1938

158. Data sourced from: "The Akamai State of the Internet Report." Akamai Technologies, 30 September 2014 and Pearson's highly regarded "Learning Curve"

159. GDP data from International Monetary Fund's World Economic Outlook for 2014

160. Pew Research Center March 19 2015. Internet Seen as Positive Influence on Education but Negative on Morality in Emerging and Developing Nations.

161. John A. Byrne on May 6, 2015, in *Poets & Quants*.

162. Ibid

163. Source: Class-Central

164. *Stanford News*, October 2015: Moocs No Panacea, by Professors John Mitchell, Candace Thille, and Mitchell Stevens

165. OECD Publishing (15 Oct. 2014).

166. The Gallup-Healthways Global Wellbeing Index uses a holistic definition of wellbeing and self-reported data from individuals across the globe to create a unique view of societies' progress on the elements that matter most to wellbeing: purpose, social, financial, community, and physical. It is the most proven, mature, and comprehensive measure of wellbeing in populations.

167. Ibid

168. BCS Policy Hub 2010

169. UN Volunteers: Inspiration in Action 2015